A GUIDE TO THE GEORGIA COAST

The Georgia Conservancy

Written and compiled by members and volunteers for
The Georgia Conservancy
711 Sandtown Road, Savannah, GA 31410

Edited by
Gwen McKee

Preface by
Eugenia Price

Illustrations by   Maps by
Carol Johnson   Suzanne McIntosh

Your purchase of this book helps fund the conservation activities of
The Georgia Conservancy, a non-profit, statewide environmental group.

The Georgia Conservancy
would like to dedicate this book
to the many volunteers who made this book a reality,
and to the Junior League of Savannah, Inc.
whose generous support made the guide possible.

First printing, February 1985
Second printing, November 1985
Revised Edition, December 1988

Library of Congress Catalog Card No. 84-073161

Illustrations by Carol Johnson
Maps by Suzanne McIntosh
Printed in the United States of America

ISBN No. 0-9614284-0-6

TABLE OF CONTENTS

PREFACE

Before beginning to write this preface, I've spent fascinating hours reading the pages that follow. Aloud, to my friend, Joyce Blackburn with whom I work and live – over and over – I said, "If only we'd had a book like this when we first found the coast of Georgia!" I meant it. Quite by accident, in the midst of a long book promotion tour back in 1961, we happened onto the wondrous land where we now make our home, with little or nothing to guide us in our exciting discovery. The hard way, through countless interviews, searches through old records, miles and miles of driving up and down the coast, we finally pieced together enough of the geography and history for me to have written the St. Simons Trilogy of novels. Not only did our search cause us to sell our Chicago home and move at once to the Georgia coast, it drastically changed both our personal and writing lives. I am at work now on my eighth novel laid here – the second in a planned quartet of novels about old Savannah. Joyce has written the biography of General Oglethorpe, Georgia's founder and will begin work soon on a biography of Juliette Gordon Low of Savannah.

Something decisive is quite apt to happen to you, too, as you begin your own treasure hunt along the Georgia coast. The natural beauty, will, of course, capture you at once. Parts of the coast are, to my Conservancy-oriented mind, over-developed, but the mystique is plainly still here. Some of us in The Georgia Conservancy were able to help a little in preserving our magical marshes, as productive in the food chain as they are breathtaking to watch. And, *do* watch the marshes in the changing, singular coastal light! To me, they rival the desert in their subtle light play. Quite naturally, when one explores the coastline, the sea with its similarly changing cloud patterns, surface and depth lights, enters the memory to stay. Still, I feel I must remind you to pay close attention to God's *microcosm* along your coastal adventure, even as you revel in His macrocosm of sea, sky, and marsh.

For example, as I sat writing these lines, Joyce came in my office holding a coastal treasure in her hand. She brought a tiny clump of moss – pale, sage green after a rain and looking, as she said, for all the world like a miniature rain forest! If you stay long enough and pay attention, you'll find an unexpected delight in examining our lichens, our hanging moss, our tiny "rain forests" and ferns that grow along old logs, on tree branches, on roofs and tombstones among the many historic cemeteries.

Directions for finding old cemeteries are to be found in this marvelous book and much about our coastal history which has so engrossed me that I know I cannot live long enough to learn all I want to know. I am proud, *proud* of our Georgia Conservancy for publishing this important volume and by the way, I strongly urge you to get a copy of my dear friend, Burnette Vanstory's excellent book, Georgia's Land of The Golden Isles for use along with A Guide to the Georgia Coast.

We welcome you to what the Indians once called "the enchanted land" and hope your adventure changes you, too. When it's time to leave – if you have to – don't feel too sad because you will have new, vivid memories which need never leave.

Eugenia Price, St. Simons Island, Georgia, November 1984

ACKNOWLEDGEMENTS

A Guide to the Georgia Coast was first conceived in the spring of 1983 as a method to achieve several key goals of The Georgia Conservancy: to educate the public on the wonderful natural resources of the coast, to encourage public support for these natural resources, and to encourage visitation to many of these rural sites in coastal Georgia.

The guide became a team effort engineered by several Georgia Conservancy volunteers, and in the spring of 1984, the guide gained momentum from the Junior League of Savannah, Inc. Providing funds and a diligent group of volunteers to assist in compiling the guide, the Junior League made this dream a reality. The cooperative efforts between the Junior League and The Georgia Conservancy have been noteworthy from the outset, for without one or the other, this guide would not have been published.

We are most grateful to the contributing authors of the guide: Cynthia Ard, Anselm Atkins, John Brower, Tee Brower, Billy Campbell, Catherine Cooper, Babs Crittenden, Les Davenport, Herb DeRigo, Anne Donnelly, Cindy Duffy, Elliot Edwards, Brendan Galloway, Matt Gilligan, Mary Beth Keane, Clermont Lee, Margie Livingston, Karen Matthews, Ken Matthews, Gwen McKee, Tom McKee, Hans Neuhauser, Alain Ratchford, Mary Helen Ray, George Rogers, Cathy Sakas, Dale Thorpe, and Pat Young.

The multitude of jobs involved in the publication and promoting of this book are like many pieces of a puzzle, all necessary for a final product. These jobs consisted of scouting, testing, legend compiling, typing, proofreading, marketing, brochure, reception, researching, copyright, graphics, bibliography, xeroxing, and telephoning. Volunteers for the Junior League and for The Georgia Conservancy accomplished these tasks.

For the countless hours faithfully spent on the various aspects of this project we would like to thank the following Junior League volunteers: Cynthia Ard, Jane Bowden, Catherine Cooper, Anne Coleman, Babs Crittenden, Cindy Duffy, Cissy Fox, Nina Gant, Wendy Jones, Mary Beth Keane, Jane Lane, Louise Lynch, Kathryn McIntosh, Pat Moss, Keller Murphy, Biddy Osbun, Helen Passavant, Alain Ratchford, Kim Reardon, Coren Ross, Ann Sheils, Linder Sipple, Mary Meade Sipple, Julia Smith, Lyndell Stanley, Dede Warren, and Linda Zoller.

We also would like to thank the many volunteers for The Georgia Conservancy who dedicated time, encouragement, and research assistance: Tina Adams, Katheryn Adler, Emily Amburgey, Anselm Atkins, Ken Atkins, Claude Black, Nancy Bland, Daniel Brown, Billy Campbell, Charles Carpenter, Chuck Cooper, John Crawford, Richard Daigle, Herb DeRigo, Phil Dew, Anne Donnelly, Elliot Edwards, Kurt Emmanuele, Jeffrey Galin, Brendan Galloway, Wade Gastin, Heidi Gilligan, Becky Griffenhagen, Margaret Hatch, Roddy Hatch, Zack Kirkland, Tom Kozel, Judy Jennings, Clermont Lee, Geraldine LeMay, Tom McKee, Bill McLaughlin, Rod McLeod, Trish McLeod, Margaret Melton, Charles Milmine, Dick Murlless,

Mary Louise Neuhauser, Bretta Perkins, Tom Porzio, Robert Redmond, Charles Reeves, William McLeod Rhodes, Cathy Sakas, Taylor Schoettle, Charles W. Seyle, Marion Shaw, Tom Stanley, Jon Streich, Lewis Taylor, Arnold Tenenbaum, Sonny Thorpe, Catharine Varnedoe, Gerry Williamson, Sharon Woods, and Pat Young.

Special thanks are extended to the National Park Service, the U.S. Fish & Wildlife Service, and the Georgia Department of Natural Resources who provided guidance and essential information for the guide.

While the responsibility for the accuracy of the information presented in the guide rests with us, we do wish to acknowledge the contributions of our reviewers: Emily Bowron, Jim Cooley, Carol Friedman, David Gillespie, Bob Humphries, Fred Marland, Becky Milmine, Albert Scardino, and Bill White.

Special thanks are necessary to Becky Shortland for supervising the production of the manuscript and for offering her valuable technical assistance and advice.

We are also grateful to Bill Morton and Randy Taylor of Miller Press for helping to guide this book through its most perilous passages.

The acknowledgements would not be complete without recognizing the contributions of our illustrators: Carol Johnson of the University of Georgia Marine Extension Service, and Suzanne McIntosh of the Skidaway Institute of Oceanography.

We, the Steering Committee, are grateful for the natural bounty of coastal Georgia that gave us the desire to produce this book.

The Steering Committee:
Dale Thorpe, chairman
Mary Hill, chairman Junior League guidebook project
Gwen McKee, co-chairman Junior League guidebook project
Karen Matthews, marketing chairman
Ken Matthews, board of trustees, The Georgia Conservancy
Hans Neuhauser, coastal director, The Georgia Conservancy
Emily Bowron, graphics chairman
Margie Livingston, executive liaison, Junior League of Savannah, Inc.
Becky Shortland, administrative assistant, The Georgia Conservancy

Barrier Islands Habitat

WELCOME TO A SPECIAL PLACE

Each traveler of the Georgia coast has the opportunity to discover an area rich in history, unusual in its ecosystems, and prized for its relative absence of the effects of man. This guide presents an introduction to this region – approximately 100 miles from South Carolina to Florida and 30 miles inland. Today's explorers of the Georgia coast can perceive – with some effort and initiative – the area's cultural history from the native American Indians to the Spanish missionaries and the colonial British. Later, the coast experienced intense exporting of timber and cotton to Europe; rice plantations prospered; and, more recently, wealthy Americans built elaborate seasonal residences. From the shell middens left by Indians thousands of years ago, to prominent military fortifications built by the British and Americans, the coast reveals an intricate pattern of natural and human history.

Many travelers have explored this coast, but their presence may speak in subtle ways. Any site, from the beach to the pine forest, may well have been marked by periods of occupation by different people in this area. Barrier islands – most of which are completely undeveloped – are some of the most captivating on the East Coast and were the sites of the earliest settlements. These islands are separated from the mainland by the salt marsh which sees the twice daily ebb and flow of a 6 to 8 foot tide.

The ecological and cultural wealth of the Georgia coast has a spellbinding quality luring visitors with moss-draped live oaks, broad tidewater rivers, and miles of white, sandy beaches. More importantly, one may be recharged by the elements of nature and by the opportunities for solitude. The Georgia coast is a wonderful place to be. While the volunteer members of The Georgia Conservancy feel an urge to share this treasure with those who would appreciate this unspoiled area, they do so with some reservations of what will be brought by the increased exposure.

The writers of this book have been guided by the objective of creating a reasonable perspective of what the visitor can expect when visiting these sites. The judgments inherent in this guide were made by the members of the steering committee of this guide all of whom live on the coast of Georgia.

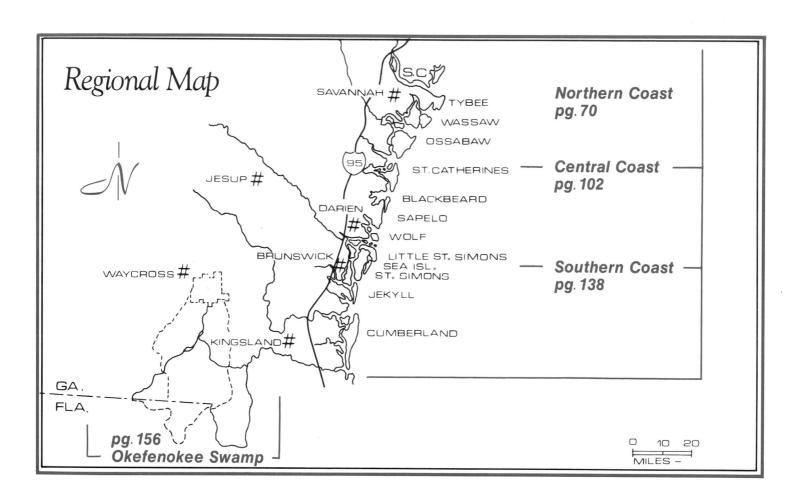

Regional Map

S.C

SAVANNAH #

TYBEE

WASSAW

OSSABAW

95

ST. CATHERINES

JESUP #

BLACKBEARD

DARIEN #

SAPELO

WOLF

BRUNSWICK #

LITTLE ST. SIMONS
SEA ISL.
ST. SIMONS

WAYCROSS #

JEKYLL

CUMBERLAND

KINGSLAND #

GA.

FLA.

**pg. 156
Okefenokee Swamp**

**Northern Coast
pg. 70**

**Central Coast
pg. 102**

**Southern Coast
pg. 138**

0   10   20
MILES –

6

What Can Be Found In This Book

This guide to 40 historical and ecological sites and 8 coastal rivers can acquaint the reader with this region and provide specific suggestions on how, where, and when to visit. The map opposite provides an overview of this area crossed by Interstate Highway 95 and U.S. Highway 17. Detailed maps of the Northern Coast, Central Coast, Southern Coast, and Okefenokee Swamp Area precede the site descriptions.

The sites included in this guide range from those areas easily accessible and well prepared for the public, such as Fort Pulaski near Savannah, to areas such as Wassaw Island with its boneyard beach accessible to only those traveling by boat. The following table provides an efficient method for helping the reader identify those sites which will be of most interest. The hiker, the bird watcher, the historian, the family with children, the touring school group, and the person who loves to walk on the beach can all scan this table to set their priorities quickly and begin their planning. A summary of the accessibility of the sites is also shown in the following table. Sites are also identified as being relatively convenient for those persons with mobility restrictions.

COASTAL GEORGIA TRIP PLANNING GUIDE

Recreational Vehicle Camping	Tent Camping	Advance Reservations Required for Access	Boat Required for Access	Accessible to Handicapped Person	Description on Page	Site	Beach Explorer	Birder	Naturalist	Bicyclist	Canoeist	Fisherman	Hiker	Historian	Family with Children	Student Group
						Northern Coast										
				✓	71	Bonaventure Cemetery		✓	✓	✓				✓		
				●	72	Fort Jackson								●	●	✓
✓	✓			✓	73	Fort McAllister		✓	✓			✓		●	●	✓
				●	75	Fort Pulaski National Monument		✓	✓			✓	✓	★	●	✓
				✓	77	Marine Extension Center			✓						✓	★
					78	New Ebenezer		✓	✓			✓	✓	✓	✓	
				✓	80	Oatland Island Education Center		✓	✓						★	●
	✓	✓	✓		81	Ossabaw Island	✓	✓	✓			✓	✓		✓	✓
				●	83	Savannah National Wildlife Refuge		●	✓	●	✓	✓	✓		✓	✓
				●	85	Savannah Science Museum			✓						●	●
		✓			87	Savannah Science Museum Ogeechee River Property		✓	✓							✓
✓	✓			✓	88	Skidaway Island State Park		✓	✓	✓		✓	✓	✓		
					89	Tuckassee King Landing		✓	✓		✓	✓	✓	✓		
✓	✓			✓	90	Tybee Island	✓	✓	✓	✓		✓		✓	●	✓
			✓		93	Tybee National Wildlife Refuge		✓	✓							
			✓		95	Wassaw National Wildlife Refuge	●	✓	●			✓	✓		✓	✓
			✓		97	Williamson Island	✓	✓	✓							
				✓	99	Wormsloe Historic Site		✓	✓			✓	✓	✓	✓	✓

ACCESS						SITES	OF INTEREST TO									
Recreational Vehicle Camping	Tent Camping	Advance Reservations Required for Access	Boat Required for Access	Accessible to Handicapped Person	Description on Page	COASTAL GEORGIA TRIP PLANNING GUIDE	Beach Explorer	Birder	Naturalist	Bicyclist	Canoeist	Fisherman	Hiker	Historian	Family with Children	Student Group
						Central Coast										
	✓				103	Altamaha River Waterfowl Area		●	✓		✓	★		✓		✓
			✓		107	Blackbeard Island National Wildlife Refuge	✓	✓	✓			●	●			
	✓				110	Fort Barrington, the road to			●				✓	✓		
				✓	112	Fort King George			✓					●	✓	✓
			✓		114	Gray's Reef National Marine Sanctuary		●				●				✓
				●	117	Harris Neck National Wildlife Refuge		●	✓	✓		✓	✓		✓	✓
				✓	119	Hofwyl-Broadfield Plantation		✓	✓					✓	✓	✓
					121	Le Conte-Woodmanston		✓	✓			✓		✓		
	✓	✓	✓F		123	Little St. Simons Island	●	★	✓		●	✓	●	✓		
					125	Midway								●	✓	✓
	✓	✓	✓		127	St. Catherines Island	✓	✓	✓			✓	✓	✓	✓	✓
	✓	✓	✓F		129	Sapelo Island		✓	●			✓	✓	✓	✓	●
				✓	133	Sunbury Historic Site		✓	✓	✓				✓	✓	✓
			✓		135	Wolf Island National Wildlife Refuge	✓	✓	✓			✓				
						Southern Coast										
✓	✓			✓	139	Crooked River State Park		✓	✓	✓		✓			✓	✓
	✓	✓	✓F		141	Cumberland Island National Seashore	★	●	●			✓	★	✓	●	✓
✓	✓			●	144	Jekyll Island	✓	✓	✓	★		✓	✓	✓	●	✓

ACCESS						SITES	OF INTEREST TO									
Recreational Vehicle Camping	Tent Camping	Advance Reservations Required for Access	Boat Required for Access	Accessible to Handicapped Person	Description on Page	**COASTAL GEORGIA TRIP PLANNING GUIDE**	Beach Explorer	Birder	Naturalist	Bicyclist	Canoeist	Fisherman	Hiker	Historian	Family with Children	Student Group
				✓	147	Overlook Park and D.N.R. Exhibit Room		✓	✓			✓			✓	
				✓	148	St. Simons Island	✓	✓	✓	•		✓		•	✓	✓
		✓			153	Sea Island	✓	✓	✓	✓		✓			✓	
						Okefenokee Swamp Area										
					157	Okefenokee Swamp										
				✓	161	Okefenokee Swamp Park		✓	✓			✓		✓	•	✓
✓	✓			✓	162	Stephen Foster State Park		•	•		•	•			✓	•
	✓			✓	163	Suwannee Canal Recreation Area		•	★		★	✓			✓	•
✓	✓			✓	164	Laura S. Walker State Park		✓			✓	✓			✓	✓

Key:

★ = best for these activities based on accessibility, the extent of interpretation provided and overall quality of the site

● = better

✓ = present at site

F = ferry available with advance reservation

The next section of this guide provides an introduction to the unique ecological communities which the visitor will encounter along the coast, such as the beach, the marsh, and the tidal river. Not included in this book are guides to Historic Savannah, Darien, Old Town Brunswick, or the City of St. Marys. Visitor centers with guided tours or published tour guides are more readily available at these cities. The purpose of this guide is to reveal the less obvious and the less accessible features of the coast, with the expectation that few visitors would want to exclude the historic cities from their visit and would have little trouble making the necessary arrangements through the appropriate Chambers of Commerce.

How To Get There

U.S. Hwy. 17, the predecessor of Interstate 95, parallels the interstate and provides excellent access to many of the sites detailed in this guide. The traveler who is bored with interstate highways will find U.S. Hwy. 17 a practical alternative for traversing part or all of the Georgia coast. However, the exits on I-95 are convenient to areas of interest all along the coast. This guide also contains an interpretive tour of I-95, as well as a driving tour of the Bartram Trail.

Marinas are in operation at a number of locations on the coast to provide access to the tidal rivers and barrier islands (see appendix for phone numbers and addresses). These marinas are usually convenient to popular fishing areas or barrier islands. The operators of these marinas and fish camps can be excellent sources of advice on navigation, weather, and boat travel time, as well as the obvious, fishing. Many of these can also arrange to transport those who are not familiar with saltwater. The six to eight foot tides along the Georgia coast create strong currents, and frequently changing channels have embarrassed and even threatened the lives of those unprepared and inexperienced. A traveler operating his own boat would be wise to proceed with caution, study the navigation charts, stay away from open sounds, carry a VHF marine radio, and allow more than adequate time for the round trip.

How To Use The Site Descriptions

Having identified what places seem to meet their interests, the readers should then review the detailed information on each site, such as how to reach the site, how arrangements should be made, what costs can be expected, where to obtain additional information, and what to bring.

Each site description has two parts: key reference information in the legend, and a narrative to provide an introduction that may stimulate the visitor's interest. The legend provides essential information at a glance, such as phone number, fee, facilities available, hours of operation and location. The writers have tried to make the list complete for the convenience of the traveler. A list of sites has been chosen in the Georgia coastal region which are open to the public year-round, by special permission, or by prearrangement. Please pay close attention to the legend for this information so as not to expect ready admission to a place that requires advance arrangements. This information is current as of October, 1984.

Consider The Seasons, The Climate and The Insects
Palmettos and Spanish moss will tell a visitor that the subtropical climate of Florida reaches up the coast of Georgia and continues into South Carolina. In winter temperatures below freezing occur infrequently and are of short duration. Summer climate is usually hot and humid, especially in July and August. For those who prefer a more precise and quantitative description, the following table of temperatures will help in scheduling a visit.

Because of the variation in the climate, March through June, and September through November are the most popular seasons for a visit to the coast. The fall is clearly the most active saltwater fishing period, since the change in the air temperature precedes the change in water temperature. Crabbing and shrimping are best in the late summer and fall.

As the preceding temperature table indicates, the average temperature range during December, January, and February is from an early morning low of 40 degrees to a high during the afternoon of 60 degrees. This can be a wonderful time of year to experience the coast and enjoy the genuine solitude one feels when alone with the surf and wind. But a typical winter day on the Georgia coast can bring variable weather. The winter visitor should be sure to dress in layers that could be peeled off if the weather warms throughout the day. A person leaving the

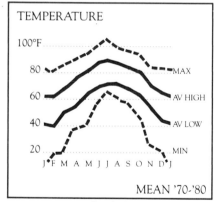

TEMPERATURE

Kinsey, B. (1982) A Sapelo Island Handbook,
University of Ga. Marine Institute, Sapelo Island

mainland during this season would be wise to carry protection from the wind for the body and head.

The coastal visitor also needs to consider insects and snakes during warm weather months, generally April through September. Heeding the following words of advice, these can be only minor irritations. Without proper precautions, however, the insects could easily disrupt a visit to many of the sites in this guide. The pleasant spring and fall weather can be interrupted by the emergence of *sand gnats* which can often be avoided by visiting open areas (beaches, waterways, or cleared areas) during breezy times. These insects seem to prefer the middle of the day when air temperatures are higher. In any case, the visitor should be aware of local tricks, such as an Avon product called "Skin So Soft," a repellent named "Claubo," or several other products which may not be quite as offensive to people. These products are frequently available in local sporting goods or hardware stores, but some convenience stores may also stock these repellents. While *mosquitos* reproduce most heavily during the summer, they can exist in wooded areas throughout the year. The hatching of mosquitos usually follows periods of heavy rain by about one week.

Chiggers and ticks are usually found in high grass and heavily wooded areas from April to October, and their presence is not felt until the scratching begins a few hours later. Chiggers cannot be seen by the human eye, but they cause a great deal of prolonged itching which can last for several days. A good spraying of insect repellent around shoes, ankles, socks, pants, and legs will generally ward off ticks and chiggers.

Poisonous and non-poisonous snakes inhabit many of the sites, but encountering a poisonous snake is an unusual occurrence. Caution should be observed when walking through the woods, tall grass, or the edge of low wet areas and interdune meadows. Snakes are cautious creatures and will bite only when antagonized, stepped on, or surprised. The majority of serious snake bites have occurred when a snake is mishandled. However, it is best to be careful around any snake and try to exercise reasonable caution in areas where snakes are most likely to be. If there is some doubt about an area hosting poisonous snakes, stay on cleared trails.

Alligators may be present in large or small numbers at almost every site in the guide. Please do not feed these alligators or encourage them to get too close. They can pose a danger, but when left alone will generally not be a threat. Hold on to children, keep dogs on a leash, and do not swim in an area that may contain alligators. Water is the alligator's natural habitat, and although an attack on humans is extremely rare, it can happen.

There are several situations infrequently experienced by visitors that should be mentioned. During the months of November through March, the air temperature over land may be very pleasant and could mislead someone who plans to spend the day boating. During these months, saltwater spray and wind may combine to produce seriously chilling conditions for those who have inadequate clothing available onboard. Another situation deserving mention is the approach of a hurricane which can bring strong winds and several days of heavy rain. These occur most frequently in the fall and are carefully tracked and reported by the weather service. Islands may need to be evacuated well before a hurricane approaches, because the unusually high tides that can coincide with the storm's arrival often flood highways and prevent a last minute departure to higher ground.

Visitors will find many interesting sites, such as the forts, readily accessible with little advance planning. Other special places well worth a little extra effort and planning, such as Cumberland Island or the Okefenokee Swamp, are on the top of many visitors' lists of unforgettable experiences. The number and variety of experiences available on the Georgia coast can hardly be absorbed in one or even a few visits. This guide should help those who come to the coast again and again to broaden their understanding of this special place.

NATURAL COMMUNITIES
OF COASTAL GEORGIA

Carol Johnson
'84

Estuaries and Sounds Habitat

NATURAL COMMUNITIES OF COASTAL GEORGIA

The purpose of this section is to present in some detail the major natural communities found in the geographic area covered by this book. Coastal Georgia is endowed with a variety of rich and diverse environments.

On the geologic calendar, Georgia's coast is quite young. At the height of the last ice age, some 15,000 years ago, the coastline was located about 95 miles east of its present location. When the first native Americans reached this coast, perhaps 10 to 12 thousand years ago, they may have gathered oysters and fish from tidal creeks that are now under 60 feet of water.

Over the eons, the Coastal Plain has been formed from sediments eroded from the Appalachian highlands. These sediments are transported to the coast by the alluvial rivers such as the Savannah and the Altamaha. There they are deposited and reworked constantly by the action of wind, tides, and ocean currents. Periodic rises and falls in sea level create a shoreline slowly but constantly migrating.

The most dynamic and youngest portions of the coast are the barrier islands. Though parts of some of these islands date back to the ice age or Pleistocene period 40,000 years ago, most have been formed during the Holocene period within the past 5,000 years. Some islands, such as Williamson, are being formed even today, influenced by the same forces which have been at work for millions of years.

Evidence of prior shorelines is seen in a series of inland sand ridges which parallel the present coast. Many of these old dune systems are prominent Indian trails and have become present-day highways. Savannah, Brunswick, and Darien are located on old sand ridges. Trail Ridge, located in extreme southeast Georgia, disrupts the drainage of this portion of the state, and forms the eastern boundary of the Okefenokee Swamp.

The Georgia coast has been divided into natural communities or ecosystems. They are (1) coastal marine, (2) barrier islands, (3) estuaries and sounds, (4) mainland upland, (5) rivers,

Ecosystems: *"Living organisms and their non-living environment, inseparably interrelated and interacting upon each other."*

Odum, *Fundamentals of Ecology*

and (6) swamps. Each has its own distinctive features, its own flora and fauna. This guide seeks to identify these major ecosystems at a moderate level of complexity and detail. Readers desiring a more detailed description are encouraged to consult Charles H. Wharton's book, The Natural Environments of Georgia.

The following pages describe the characteristics of each of these ecosystems, starting with coastal marine and moving inland. These natural communitites are of immeasurable value, and each reflects to some extent the hand of modern civilization.

COASTAL MARINE

An outstanding exhibit on the coastal marine environment may be seen at the University of Georgia's Marine Extension Center on Skidaway Island. Other good examples may be found in the Georgia Department of Natural Resources Exhibit Room in Brunswick, and at Gray's Reef National Marine Sanctuary approximately 17.5 nautical miles offshore.

A broad continental shelf slopes gradually for about 95 miles east of Georgia's shoreline to a point where the continental shelf breaks into a steep slope, descending first to the Blake Plateau (600-3000 feet deep) and then to the ocean's abyssal depths. Within this continental shelf lies the coastal marine ecosystem, between the coastal barrier islands and the Gulf Stream.

At the rate of about four miles per hour, the Gulf Stream flows from south to north 80 to 120 miles off the Georgia coast. The Gulf Stream frequently spawns smaller currents into the coastal marine ecosystem. These currents and eddies often have a subtle but important role in the movement of nutrients and organisms in nearshore waters. Also flowing off the coast, but in the opposite direction of the Gulf Stream, is the longshore current. It flows from north to south just off the barrier islands and is an important force in shaping the islands and the sounds.

There are two natural divisions within the coastal marine ecosystem: sandy bottoms and hard bottoms. The sandy bottom area appears to be an aquatic desert. Shifting sand prevents plants and non-moving animals from settling permanently. Immobile plants and animals, such as

18

sponges, coral, eel-grass, or oysters, would be buried beneath the rapidly changing bottom. The food chains that do exist in the area start not from bottom-dwelling plants but from microscopic plants, called phytoplankton, that float in the water near the surface.

Occasionally, the sandy shelf is interrupted by hard limestone outcroppings on the sea floor. These hard bottom reefs run in ridges roughly parallel to the coast in water from 60 feet to 300 feet in depth. Each hard bottom is an oasis, the only place where plants and animals can settle and attach themselves. These attached organisms in turn provide food for small fish, which in turn become food for larger fish including grouper, mackerel, amberjack, and cobia. These areas are referred to as "live bottoms" because of the relative abundance of plant and animal life.

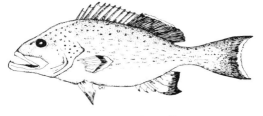

Scamp Grouper

Because naturally occurring hard bottoms are some distance off the Georgia coast, the Georgia Department of Natural Resources and sport fishing groups have created artificial reefs by sinking large barges, World War II liberty ships, and other solid material which encourages the growth of marine creatures including corals, sea whips, barnacles, oysters, crabs, small fish, and game fish.

Gray's Reef, Georgia's most well-known and accessible natural reef, is on a limestone outcrop located east of Sapelo Island. Because a natural hard bottom area like Gray's Reef is uncommon, it has been protected by the federal government as a National Marine Sanctuary. Gray's Reef's abundant plant and animal life depend on sunlight penetrating the 65 feet of water above it. Sunlight is the source of energy for photosynthesis, the starting point for coastal marine food chains. If water clouding pollutants are put into the marine water, photosynthesis could be reduced to the point that Gray's Reef would be destroyed. A major oil spill or the side effects of offshore mining for phosphates and other mineral deposits could also upset the precarious existence of the reef and spell its demise.

The coastal marine waters provide habitat for a number of oceanic birds, sea turtles, and marine mammals. Right whales, one of the most endangered of the large whales, migrate into these waters during winter months. Also, females are known to calve here, making these waters even more important for the long-term survival of the species.

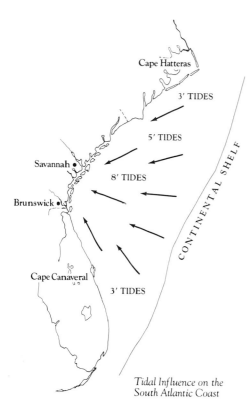

Barrier islands are those islands bordered on one side by tidal marshes, creeks, and rivers and on the other side by beaches formed by the ocean's waves.

Cape Hatteras

3' TIDES

5' TIDES

Savannah •

8' TIDES

Brunswick •

Cape Canaveral •

3' TIDES

CONTINENTAL SHELF

*Tidal Influence on the
South Atlantic Coast*

BARRIER ISLANDS

For natural features, ease of access, and availability of interpretive information on the barrier island environment, nothing exceeds Cumberland Island National Seashore. Other excellent examples include Sapelo Island, and Little St. Simons Island.

Georgia's coastline is richly endowed with barrier islands. Among these are Tybee Island, Wassaw Island, Ossabaw Island, St. Catherines Island, Blackbeard Island, Sapelo Island, Sea Island, St. Simons Island, Jekyll Island, and Cumberland Island.

These islands are called "barrier" islands because they form the shore's first line of defense against the storms and hurricanes that come sweeping out of the ocean. It is important to recognize that barrier islands are not just pieces of the mainland surrounded by water. Unlike the mainland, barrier islands are dynamic – continually changing, some eroding, some growing, some doing both simultaneously. They are extremely vulnerable to weather and to people.

Each barrier island is unique in its physical, biological, and cultural attributes. Each island is exposed to strong physical forces which include waves, tides, currents, salt spray, and sea level rise. The most important force molding the islands is the tide. On other parts of the United States coast, such as North Carolina, the dominant force is wave energy, but in Georgia the tides are dominant.

The Georgia coast forms the western end of a giant funnel. Because of this, tides rise faster and higher than elsewhere on the southeastern seaboard. The average tide on the Georgia Coast is 6 to 8 feet. In contrast, tides in North Carolina, on the northern rim of the funnel, are much smaller, generally 2 or 3 feet. Tides in Miami, on the southern rim of the funnel, are also much smaller.

Because of Georgia's high tides, there is tremendous movement of water twice a day as the tides rise and fall. Water rises in and around the barrier islands, through the sounds, and into the marshes. The tides are responsible for the flushing of the estuaries which helps create the rich environment. The tides also shape the barrier islands.

Along the Georgia coast the longshore current runs north to south and very close to the shore. The shape of the islands is largely determined by this longshore current and the twice-daily pulses of the tide. Between the barrier islands are sounds, such as Wassaw, Ossabaw, and St. Andrews. The water that is pumped in and out of these sounds deflects the longshore current and causes a great deal of turbulence where these two currents meet. Here sandbars settle in a fairly predictable yet constantly changing manner. When wind currents are added to this nature-shaping recipe, the result is the formation of a barrier island in a shape very much like a turkey drumstick. The ideal shape of barrier islands on the Georgia coast is wide and bulbous at the northern end and long and narrow towards the southern end.

When compared to the mainland, the barrier islands are geologically very young. Some, such as Sapelo, St. Simons, and most of Jekyll and Cumberland, came into existence between 25,000 to 35,000 years ago. Others, such as Tybee, Wassaw, Blackbeard, and Sea Island, were established within the last five thousand years. The older islands are flat with well developed soils, whereas the younger islands have many dune ridges and poor soil. Some islands on the Georgia coast are even younger. Fifteen miles east of Savannah is Williamson Island, a small island that did not exist 25 years ago.

Several smaller ecosystems are present on barrier islands: offshore sandbars, beach dunes, interdune meadows, maritime forests, and fresh and brackish water ponds.

Offshore Sandbars
The most complex example of offshore sandbars may be viewed at the northeastern edge of Little St. Simons Island. Other good examples are East Beach of St. Simons Island, and the northeast tip of Wassaw Island.

Sandbars take several different forms on the Georgia coast, depending on how they are created. The most prominent, especially to the operator of a small boat just off the beaches, are the sandbars associated with sand transport around the margins of sounds at the tidal inlets. The interaction of tidal currents pulsing in and out of the sounds with the north-to-south longshore current creates areas where sand carried by either one of these currents settles onto the bottom.

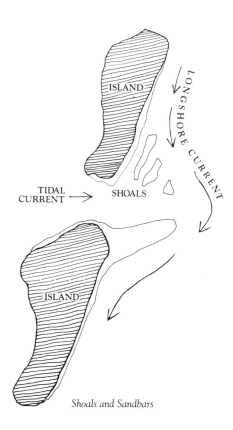

ISLAND

LONGSHORE CURRENT

TIDAL CURRENT → SHOALS

ISLAND

Shoals and Sandbars

Sometimes these sandbars become high enough to have portions remain above the level of the sea at high tide.

Other sandbars are much smaller and run parallel to the beach. They are part of the sand-sharing system that exchanges sand among the beach, the dunes, and these offshore sandbars. In addition to their importance to the integrity of the beach, offshore sandbars often serve as resting and feeding areas for shorebirds – pelicans, gulls, dunlins, terns, willets, and a variety of "peeps" (small shorebirds that appear identical and take careful observation and a knowledge of birds to distinguish).

Low tide will reveal an astonishing puzzle of sandbars that will often lure beachcombers in search of shells. The adventurer should be aware of the power of the sea and the strong tidal flow. Otherwise, a swim back to shore or to a boat, once the tide has turned, may be quite exhausting and sometimes fatal if the currents prove too swift to combat.

Sandbars, when they extend above high tide, are often used by terns and skimmers for nesting. These nesting grounds are vulnerable to human abuse. Even a casual walk through or near the nesting area will keep the adult birds off the nest for a long enough period of time for the hot summer sun to destroy the eggs or young. Because of the fragility of these nesting areas, people should not visit them during the nesting season from March to July. The visitor should watch for posted signs on Sapelo, Cumberland, and other islands and respect their message.

A careful observer will note that these sandbars and the adjacent inlets change frequently. This should serve as a reminder that the beach is simply a large sandbar with dunes on which vegetation has grown, and it also is constantly shifting and changing.

Beach Dunes

The most extensive natural beach dunes are found on Nannygoat Beach of Sapelo Island. The beach dunes on Cumberland are impressive, but show signs of abuse from pigs, horses, and cows. The dunes on Jekyll Island south of the south beach picnic area are also worth a visit.

Sand dunes are a key feature of barrier islands. Initially, dunes are formed through the accumulation of dead marsh grass, which is produced in the estuary behind the island. When the grass dies, many of the stalks wash out of the estuary on the ebb tide, then wash up on the beach. Spring high tides push the dead grass into rows along the upper margin of the beach called marshwrack. Seeds washed in by the tides or blown along the beach by the wind collect in these piles of dead marsh grass. The dead grass changes the environmental conditions underneath the piles to allow seeds from particularly hardy species of plants to germinate successfully. The grass maintains moisture, shelters the seeds from the wind, insulates the seeds, moderates temperature, and retains organic materials and nutrients from which the young plants can gain sustenance.

The physical forces of salt spray, occasional inundation by high tides, and shifting sands allow only the hardiest of plants to survive. These are called pioneer plants because they can tolerate very harsh conditions and colonize a previously barren area. Just like the pioneers of the American frontier, the plants modify the habitat in which they grow. Eventually, the habitat changes and the pioneers can no longer compete with the new arrivals. The new arrivals would not be successful, though, without the habitat changes brought about by the pioneer plants.

These ocean front plants provide a good example of the interaction between the living and non-living parts of the environment. As the plants grow up through the sand, sand grains blown up from the beach are caught behind the plants just as a snow fence catches snow behind it. As the sand accumulates, some of the early pioneers are covered. New arrivals such as the sea oats are able to grow up rapidly through the sand. This new growth accumulates more sand. The result is the formation of a sand dune stabilized by sea oats and other plants.

The unique root system of the sea oats and its important role in stabilizing the sand dunes was not recognized until recently. The attractive plume of the sea oat that sways so gently in the breeze became a souvenir of many a tourist who wanted to carry something of the beach back home. In danger of being over-picked, thereby allowing destabilization of the dune, the sea oat is now protected by law. Sea oats should not be picked on any Georgia beach.

Trampling of dunes has the same effect. Even one careless visitor walking through the dunes can cause significant damage to their stability.

Sea Oats

The sand dunes play a vital role in maintaining the sandsharing system. During a storm, particularly those generated during the winter, the beach and dunes lose their sand to the offshore bars. At the return of calm weather, the sand from the bar is gradually washed back onto the beach. Some of that sand then gets trapped in the dead marsh grass at the high tide line and the dune building process starts again. Often one can see a straight windrow of marshwrack, and if sufficient windblown sand is available, a new dune ridge may form.

Erosion and accretion of beaches is a constant phenomenon. On most islands, erosion and accretion are happening simultaneously on different parts of the beach. For instance, part of Ossabaw Island's beach is eroding while another part is building up. While erosion is a natural phenomenon, intervention, especially with seawalls, jetties, dredging of harbor channels, and other sand-robbing activities, often accentuates the erosion.

When a wave crashes into a sea wall, the energy contained in that wave has three ways to go: up, as salt spray, straight ahead into the wall, or down. The wave energy moving down scours out the sand at the base of the wall, at first creating a water-filled pit. Eventually the erosion requires the reinforcement of the first seawall with another wall and then another. Soon there is no beach left at all.

To foster commerce at the ports, navigation channels have been dredged between barrier islands. The sand that flows along our coast, suspended in the water of the longshore currents, falls into these channels instead of winding up on the next beach to the south. The loss of sand on islands south of navigation channels is often dramatic.

The animals and plants that survive on the barrier islands are those that can respond to this continually changing environment. Two survival techniques are evident on the beach front. One is that of a transient. When conditions on the beach are favorable, animals such as crabs, raccoons, or shorebirds move in to feed, rest, or nest. When conditions are unfavorable, these animals leave. If a young royal tern is drowned by an abnormally high tide or storm, the adults can usually find another place and nest again during the same season.

The other survival technique exhibited on the beach is that of burrowing down into the sand to avoid the harsh conditions of the beach surface. Ghost crabs, clams, and sand dollars

Whelk Egg Case

illustrate the burrowing strategy. Another is the ghost shrimp. This animal lives in burrows about a foot or more below the surface of the beach, but the burrow openings are easily observed near the low tide line. The openings are about the size of pencil lead and are often surrounded by small cylindrical gray or brown fecal pellets.

The loggerhead sea turtle, with a maximum weight of 800 pounds and length up to 42 inches, is the only marine turtle which regularly nests on Georgia's coast. Average females in Georgia weigh 150-300 pounds and attain a length of 36 inches. Turtles only come out of the sea to nest. A nest shaped like a lightbulb is excavated in the dune area, and there the female deposits an average of 120 leathery-shelled eggs, each about the size of a ping pong ball. The female then returns to the ocean, leaving the eggs to hatch on their own. One female may nest up to six times in a season, but she only nests every two or three years. The largest threats to the eggs come from raccoons, erosion, and man. Loggerhead sea turtle eggs take about two months to hatch.

Currently classified as a threatened species, these large reptiles face more immediate threats to their survival. Accidental drownings in commercial shrimpers' nets and development of beach front property could spell their demise. However, the recent introduction of turtle proof shrimp nets and the efforts of turtle research and hatchery projects like Wassaw Island's Caretta Project will hopefully ensure the survival of these ancient creatures.

In the past the presence of humans on barrier islands has been traditionally transient. But people have acquired more leisure time and discretionary dollars; thus, humans are now permanent fixtures on the shore. Attitudes towards barrier islands must change. The concept of being a transient should once again be embraced. When building occurs, the dunes should be protected. Boardwalks should be provided for crossing the dunes, and they should be constructed in such a way as to maintain the sandsharing system. Where buildings are necessary, they should be behind the dunes, on parts of the island that are unlikely to erode rapidly. If erosion does threaten a building, it should be removed or allowed to fall into the ocean. Construction must be in cooperation with nature, not independent of nature. If this is not done, the environment will prevail: the structure will be naturally destroyed, or exorbitant sums will be spent to save it.

Loggerhead Sea Turtle

Report any strandings or sightings of sea turtles, whales, or manatees to:
GA Dept. of Natural Resources
912/264-7218

On those islands where the errors of the past have already been committed, responses to change should be as compatible with natural processes as possible. Because the undeveloped barrier islands of Georgia are still responding to natural forces, they provide a prime source for the study of erosion and rapidly rising sea level, currently estimated at 13 inches a century.

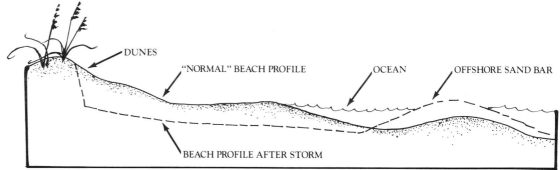

Sand Sharing System

Interdune Meadows
The best place to view interdune meadows is on Nannygoat Beach on Sapelo Island. A close second is at Sea Camp on Cumberland Island National Seashore.

On a growing beach there are often three or more rows of sand dunes. The innermost dune is the oldest, supporting a greater variety of vegetation, and the outer dune is the youngest, supporting only a few hardy species of vegetation as it continues to grow and establish itself.

If a stretch of beach has been able to grow for an appreciable length of time, then the sequence of events that leads to the formation of sand dunes has had an opportunity to occur more than once. Younger dunes develop between the beach and the older dunes, creating a dune field. These dune fields consist of roughly parallel rows of dunes interspersed with interdune meadows.

The youngest dunes, closest to the ocean, are usually covered with pioneer plants. Slightly older dunes are covered with sea oats. Often near their bases are shorter grasses and dune sandspurs. The latter plant is named for its seedpods that will stick to anything and make walking barefoot a most unpleasant experience. The older dunes are also covered with sea oats, but there has been enough time for other salt-tolerant species to become established. Still older dunes may have been around long enough for live oak trees and cabbage palmettos to grow.

In between the dunes are the interdune meadows. The grasses and shrubs that grow here must be able to withstand regular exposure to salt spray. Wax myrtle shrubs are commonly found here, along with pennywort, broomsedge and other grasses.

Wax Myrtle

Occasionally, as the result of storm wave surges or erosion, the dunes are breached, and saltwater floods the interdune meadow. Such an event generally kills the wax myrtle and covers many of the smaller plants with sand and debris. But if the sea retreats, the area will eventually recover.

The interdune meadows are frequented by animals such as marsh rabbits and small native rats. These, in turn, are prey for snakes, including the eastern diamondback rattlesnake. Moles live here too, and their burrows just below the surface of the sand are a common occurrence.

Interdune meadows are particularly obvious on islands that are growing. On the developed islands, these areas become favorite places to build condominiums, so it is difficult to find an intact interdune meadow and dune field on islands like Tybee and St. Simons.

Maritime Forest
The least disturbed maritime forest may be found on Wassaw National Wildlife Refuge. Another good example is on Cumberland Island National Seashore.

Behind the beach and the interdune meadows lies the maritime forest. Well developed on the sea islands of South Carolina and Georgia, this forest is not typical on islands that are washed over frequently by storm waves, such as the Outer Banks of North Carolina.

Influence of Salt Spray on Maritime Forest.

The maritime forest is also affected by the salt spray from the ocean. Often the forest canopy appears to be manicured and shaped by the spray. Trees close to the ocean are often stunted,

27

and their branches and leaves are pruned by the wind. Few plants can tolerate this salt spray; but once out of the spray, plant life becomes more diverse. The live oak is dominant in the maritime forest, but pine, redbay, wax myrtle, cabbage palmetto, saw palmetto, Southern magnolia, holly, and tupelo are often seen. Spanish moss, muscadine grape, and resurrection fern enhance the natural beauty of the trees and give the forest the romantic look of the South.

Spanish moss grows in profusion within the maritime forest. Its luxuriant growth on the coast is occasionally interrupted by a blight of unknown origin. This plant is neither Spanish nor a moss; it's a member of the family which includes bromeliads and pineapple. In spring one can often detect a small inconspicuous flower. Most often seen draped from the branches of live oak trees, Spanish moss is not a parasite, but rather an epiphyte. The moss derives its nutrients from the air. Occasionally, however, it gets so thick it may hamper the growth and vigor of some trees.

Spanish moss provides a habitat for parula warblers, yellow-throated warblers, and painted buntings. To spot the shy, male painted bunting within the forest is a particular treat, for the colors rival an artist's palette with its red, blue, yellow, and green feathers. Spanish moss at one time was often harvested in the southeast for stuffing sofas and chairs. Spanish moss can serve as a roosting site for several different kinds of bats.

Resurrection fern, so named because of its ability to arise from a seemingly dead state after a rain shower, is quite prevalent on the branches of live oak trees.

The isolation created by the island environment also has an effect on the types and number of animals that live there. Genetic exchange among animals is limited. The resulting inbreeding favors the evolution of animals which have characteristics different from their mainland ancestors. Island populations are sometimes recognized as distinct genetic entities, and currently there are four such forms that are restricted primarily to one or more of Georgia's barrier islands: the Cumberland Island pocket gopher, the Anastasia Island cotton mouse, the St. Simons Island raccoon, and the Blackbeard Island deer.

Resurrection Fern and Spanish Moss on Live Oak Tree.

The isolation also influences the number of different types of animals and plants that live on the islands. For example, there are six species of poisonous snakes found in coastal Georgia, but only two are usually found on the barrier islands, the eastern diamondback rattlesnake, and cottonmouth.

Fresh and Brackish Water Ponds

Little St. Simons Island is an outstanding place to see fresh and brackish water ponds. Good examples may also be seen behind the dunes on the northern half of Cumberland Island National Seashore and in the interior of both Wassaw and Blackbeard Island National Wildlife Refuges.

On most of the barrier islands there are fresh and brackish water ponds many of which are man-made. Brackish water is a mixture of salt water and fresh water. The amount of salt in the water depends on how frequently the pond is breached by storm waves, how much evaporation there has been, how much rain has fallen, and how much salt spray the pond receives. Some plants and animals are highly tolerant of variations of salt content, while others, such as cattails, are not.

If not disrupted by fire or periodic inundation by saltwater, ponds would gradually fill and the vegetation would change, eventually becoming part of the maritime forest. But fires ignited by lightning occur often enough to burn away accumulated vegetation, and salt water floods the ponds often enough to inhibit plant growth.

There are many more ponds on the islands that appear and disappear with rainfall. These ponds are most prevalent between the parallel stretches of sand dune ridges on the younger islands. Older islands have been around long enough for their sand dunes to erode away, leaving only a flat plain instead of a shallow pond.

Ponds are the only major source of freshwater available to island wildlife. There are no rivers on the islands, and streams are limited to pond drainage during periods of heavy rain when ponds overflow into lower areas. These ponds play a major role in maintaining some of the more interesting wildlife on the islands, notably alligators and wading birds.

In the fall, ponds are important resting and feeding areas for migrating and wintering water-fowl. These birds feed on acorns and fruit from adjacent trees as well as upon aquatic plants.

In the spring, many herons, egrets, and other wading birds form nesting colonies or rookeries in the ponds. Often, fledglings fall into the water, providing food for alligators and cotton-mouth snakes. Understandably, dense populations of these reptiles may build up on ponds having numerous colonies of nesting birds.

Grasses, duckweed, and microscopic algae, which capture the energy of the sun, serve as food for small fish, grass shrimp, and tadpoles, which in turn are a food source for birds, raccoons, and other predators. Populations of a number of animals, particularly frogs, are highly dependent on the availability of ponds. A wet season, a dark night, and spring weather will provide a setting for a deafening chorus of various species of frogs.

When a pond starts to dry up, its inhabitants are concentrated in the remaining water. These densely populated areas become feeding grounds for turtles and birds such as the endangered wood stork. Ponds, while not extensive on any barrier island, add appreciably to the island's diversity.

Spartina alterniflora

ESTUARIES AND SOUNDS

A ferryboat trip from Meridian Dock to Sapelo Island provides the best opportunity to experience the estuaries and sounds of the Georgia coast. The ferryboat trip from St. Marys to Cumberland Island National Seashore provides a similar experience.

The estuarine ecosystem is the region where river and sea meet. Along the Georgia coast the rivers and estuaries flow into the sounds that separate the barrier islands. Therefore, the seawater in these sounds is diluted with freshwater from the rivers.

Ocean tides play an important role in the estuarine ecosystem. In addition to shaping the barrier islands, the tidal action provides the nutrients for plants that live in the estuaries behind the barrier islands.

The estuaries and sounds of coastal Georgia are comprised of two major parts — that part which is always under water (subtidal) and that part which is periodically flooded and exposed (intertidal).

Salt Marsh and Intertidal Creek Banks

There are many places on the coast to view the extensive salt marshes from a distance, but a visit to Sapelo Island National Estuarine Research Reserve provides an opportunity to get close, to keep shoes dry, and still learn a lot about this valuable yet vulnerable environment. Other places to learn about the marsh include Fort Pulaski National Monument, Oatland Island Education Center, and Overlook Park. For school groups, the best place for a "hands-on" experience is at the Marine Extension Center, but reservations for this are necessary.

The salt marsh is the most dramatic or prominent feature of the intertidal estuarine area. It is also the most characteristic feature of Georgia's coastal environment. Lying between the barrier islands and the Georgia mainland is a wide band of marshland covering approximately 400,000 acres. This band of marsh varies in width from about one mile near Cumberland Island to ten miles of marsh separating Tybee from the mainland. Georgia and South Carolina together have more than 50% of the East Coast's salt marshes.

The slowly subsiding coastline, rising sea level, and the salt content of the estuarine waters have created favorable conditions for the formation of salt marshes. The vegetation within the salt marsh is influenced by elevation, soil conditions, frequency and duration of inundation, and evaporation rates.

Marsh Periwinkle

The salt marsh is a highly productive ecosystem. Scientists working at the University of Georgia's Marine Institute on Sapelo Island have been world leaders in helping to understand its value. Much of the energy that enters the marsh in the form of sunlight is captured by marsh grass and by microscopic plants that inhabit the water and the marsh mud surface. These plants and dead marsh grass play a vital role in supporting the food chains that may put shrimp, oysters, crab, or fish on the dinner table.

More than 70% of the fish and shellfish that are harvested from the waters of Georgia and South Carolina depend on the salt marsh during some or all of their life cycle. Many organisms utilize the marsh as a nursery ground. Shrimp, oyster, and crab larvae spend part of their existence in the water that flows through the base of the marsh grass. As these larvae of aquatic organisms grow, they move out into the estuary where they either settle on the bottom (oysters) or grow in the coastal waters (shrimp and crab).

The salt marsh captures essential nutrients that flow down the rivers, especially during spring floods. These nutrients are then gradually released into the environment for other organisms to use. Most of the marsh is flooded twice a day by the tides. These tides are important in helping to distribute nutrients and organic material, oxygen, and floating or swimming plants and animals.

The salt marsh is dominated by one species of grass, smooth cordgrass, also called spartina. At a distance, this grass appears to be relatively uniform in height. However, on close examination, three distinct zones can be found. Cordgrass marsh is found along creek banks, the smooth cordgrass marsh occurs on top of natural levees that line the creek banks, and short cordgrass marsh is found on higher elevations of the marsh.

In the portion of marsh that is higher in elevation and thus flooded only occasionally, the vegetation changes. Short cordgrass marsh gives way to a very short cordgrass where the most prominent resident is the fiddler crab. The slightly higher part of the marsh is dominated by glassworts and seashore saltgrass. Glasswort is good to eat; its salty-lemon taste adds a certain flair to salads. Often there are barren sand flats in this zone. These sand (or salt) flats are characterized by very high salt content and very high temperatures in the summer; this combination creates a habitat in which most species of plants cannot survive. On higher ground, but still occasionally flooded, is the black needlerush marsh. Dense stands of this grass (with needle-sharp tips) are occasionally interspersed with other salt-tolerant plants such as marsh elder and sea oxeye.

When the different marsh grasses die, but are still upright, microscopic fungi, algae, and bacteria attach to the grass and absorb its nutrients. As the grass decays, it drops to the ground

Public oyster and clam harvesting areas are now available in each coastal county. Call the Georgia Department of Natural Resources (912/264-7218) for information on location and limits.

where most deteriorates or serves as a source of food for small animals, which, in turn, become food for larger organisms.

The land animals which have adapted to living, feeding, and breeding in the marsh include the raccoon, mink, otter, rat, diamondback terrapin, clapper rail, marsh wren, and marsh rabbit.

Realization of the many values of the salt marsh and their vulnerability to abuse by people prompted the Georgia General Assembly to pass the Coastal Marshlands Protection Act in 1970. This act requires a permit for any activity altering the salt marsh. Few permits have been granted over the years that would allow extensive marsh destruction.

Governmental activities of dredging for navigation and highway construction are exempt from the permit requirements of the Coastal Marshlands Protection Act. However, federal statutes, particularly Section 404 of the Clean Water Act, require that these kinds of projects be scrutinized for their environmental impact. Generally, this scrutiny leads to minimal alteration of the marsh.

Raccoon

Tidal Creeks and Sounds

Jekyll Island offers the easiest opportunity to view examples of Georgia's sounds, at both the northern end (St. Simons Sound) and southern end (St. Andrews Sound) of the island. Sounds can also be seen from the ferryboats to Sapelo Island and Cumberland Island. The best examples of sounds essentially undisturbed by dredging and its effects may be seen between any two undeveloped barrier islands, such as Ossabaw and St. Catherines.

The best place to observe what is present in these coastal waters is at the Marine Extension Center on Skidaway Island. Also notice this ecosystem while crossing any bridge over a salt-water creek or river.

Estuarine waters, enriched by the nutrients and organic materials from the salt marsh, are teeming with life. Out of these waters commercial fishermen find their livelihood. Commercial landings of fish and shellfish at Georgia ports during 1983 exceeded seventeen million pounds valued at over twenty-five million dollars. The waters are also extremely popular for recreational fishing.

The richness of the estuary is not confined to the area behind the barrier islands. Tidal and nearshore currents help transport the nutrients and organic material out into the coastal marine environment. The density of materials can easily be observed in the form of murky water often extending several miles offshore.

Estuarine waters are not "dirty," although there are some places near industrialized zones where pollution does indeed make them "dirty." The murky color of the water is due to a combination of suspended sediments and the "vegetable soup" of decayed marsh grass and microscopic algae. Farther offshore, the water clears and sport diving becomes pleasurable.

A prominent inhabitant of the estuary is the Atlantic bottlenosed dolphin. Individuals and small groups are often seen feeding in the open estuarine waters of the coast. These are Georgia's most common marine mammal. Manatees may be seen in coastal waters, especially during warmer months of the year, but seeing one is a rare event.

Spider Crab

MAINLAND UPLAND

Many of coastal Georgia's mainland upland forests have been altered over the years, and few examples of what used to be are left. A drive down Interstate 95 will let you see a good cross section of what's here now. Other places to go include New Ebenezer, Harris Neck National Wildlife Refuge, Midway, and Crooked River State Park.

The upland ecosystem has a lower water table than the wetlands or aquatic systems. The soil is generally drier, consequently the plants are predominantly lower-moisture plants. Most of the flatlands are poorly drained and can be used for pasture or pinelands.

The activities of people have drastically altered most of the upland ecosystem. The original forests were probably a mixed hardwood forest with some pines. What is present today is almost entirely a third-growth forest. Where undisturbed, the forest matures gradually by the process of succession.

Succession is an orderly sequence of changes which occur in vegetation over a period of time. This in turn leads to the formation of a stable, self-reproducing plant community. In many parts of the world it is possible to predict with reasonable accuracy the species that will be present at what point. However, no such pattern has been determined for early succession in the outer coastal plain of the southeastern United States.

There are certain species which are fairly conspicuous in coastal Georgia. These species are likely to be present on well watered, well drained, sandy loam soil. Some of the species include white oak, American beech, laurel oak, live oak, Southern magnolia, pignut hickory, dogwood, American holly, devilwood osmanthus, sparkleberry, witch hazel, saw palmetto, fringe tree, horse sugar, redbay, chinkapin, and pawpaw.

In early succession, in most places, a mixed pine-hardwood forest is likely to form. This will then gradually be replaced by hardwoods, because the native pines cannot reproduce in shade.

The complete process of succession takes a long time, as long as 150 years in the southeast. If the process is uninterrupted, it terminates in a community which is able to reproduce and maintain itself indefinitely. This ultimate combination of plants is often referred to as the climax community. In the southeastern coastal plain the climax community is the southern mixed hardwood forest, provided there has not been fire. Where fire occurs by accident or intent, pine often is the climax forest tree, as it withstands some fire.

There are very few places in Georgia where one may see a mature southern mixed hardwood forest. Most wooded areas are in some intermediate state of succession, while many are cultivated as pine forest.

Six native species of pine occur in this region: slash, spruce, loblolly, pond, longleaf, and short leaf. Of these, the slash pine grows the fastest, and pulp and paper companies often replant slash pine after logging an area. On many of coastal Georgia's highways one will see examples of planted pine forest.

Live Oak Tree

Two places to observe a Southern mixed hardwood forest in coastal Georgia are on the property of Armstrong State College in Savannah. These two sub-climax forests are different from each other in the species of trees they support.

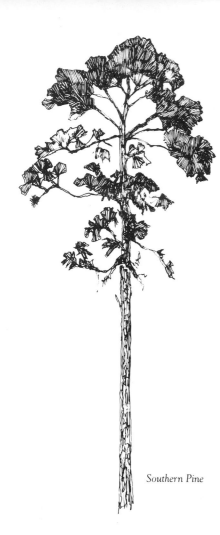

Southern Pine

The pine tree is the South's most versatile and economically important tree. Large industries are dependent on its harvest for pulp and paper products, lumber, and turpentine. Other companies use pine roots to produce chemicals.

In the lower reaches of the coastal plains of Georgia are flatwoods covered by pine forest. Intermingled among the pine forests are hardwood swamps and bays in which red maple, American elm, tupelo, and bald cypress dominate. Common flatwood shrubs are blueberry, holly, huckleberry, and wild azalea.

The forest houses a number of snakes, turtles, raccoons, squirrels, deer, and quail. Occasionally, a gray fox, wild turkey, or bobcat may also be observed. The red-cockaded woodpecker, an endangered species, is dependent on large stands of old longleaf pine for its nesting sites.

RIVERS

The easiest place to see one of Georgia's outstanding river environments is on Interstate 95 as it crosses the Altamaha River. Other outstanding examples include the Suwannee, the Satilla, the Ogeechee, and the Savannah.

There are three major types of river environments in coastal Georgia: blackwater rivers, alluvial rivers, and tidewater rivers. This section will include the rivers with their associated flood plains and freshwater swamps.

Blackwater Rivers

All of the blackwater rivers in this area are outstanding with the Suwannee and the Satilla at the top. The unique biological conditions on Ebenezer Creek are also noteworthy.

Except for the larger alluvial rivers which drain the piedmont and mountainous portions of the state, most coastal rivers in Georgia are blackwater rivers. These originate in the sand and clay of the coastal plain. The name refers to the clear, tea-colored water, which in deeper areas appears black. This color is derived from the high level of organic acids leached from decomposing plant matter on the associated flood plain. The dark waters of these rivers mirror stately bald cypress and breathtaking scenery.

Characteristically, the blackwater rivers have a high organic, low silt load. The flood plain is often narrow or nonexistent. This flood plain is usually dominated by bald cypress and tupelo. Oaks, maples, and redbays are also present.

The predominant sediment in the blackwater river is sand. This sand is deposited along the riverbed forming many open sand banks and beaches which contrast with the dark waters. These are excellent streams for float or canoe trips, providing a tranquil respite for the city-weary. Water snakes and alligators are common sights, with an occasional cottonmouth. For the fisherman there is an abundance of game fish including redbreast, bluegill, large-mouth bass, and catfish.

Urban development and industrial pollution pose an ever-increasing threat to these river systems. As coastal populations increase, more pressure is placed on these resources. Channelization and impoundment are also potential sources of irreparable damage to these rivers.

Alluvial Rivers

The Altamaha, and the Savannah River upstream from the U.S. Highway 17 bridge are all excellent places to experience the alluvial river environment.

The alluvial rivers are large rivers whose headwaters originate in the mountains and piedmont of Georgia. There are two in the area covered by this guide, the Savannah River and the Altamaha River. The Ogeechee River exhibits characteristics that are intermediate between the alluvial rivers and the blackwater rivers. Alluvial rivers carry a high sediment load. A striking characteristic of alluvial rivers is their broad flood plain, generally three to twelve miles wide.

Alluvial rivers and their bottomland must be considered as a single unit. The river channel carries the flow of water approximately six months of the year. During periods of high water, however, water overflows into the flood plain or river swamp dissipating its energy over a wide area and depositing its load of sediment and minerals. Some organic material accumulated on the forest floor of the flood plain becomes suspended and is carried down river making an important contribution to the richness of the estuary and coastal marine ecosystem.

Several different terrains, each with its own flora, are found within these flood plains. Natural levees occur along the river edge. Behind these levees are deeper sloughs and oxbow lakes with permanently standing water. Flat bottomlands with varying periods of submersion each year also occur in the flood plain, and finally intermittent higher ridges. Water generally inundates the flood plain from late fall into the spring. This annual flood plays a central role in the life cycle and growth of any river and swamp dweller. The surge of water and nutrients is an important factor promoting optimal tree growth.

Bald cypress and tupelo dominate the sloughs and lakes. Higher portions of the flood plain with shorter periods of inundation support tupelos, oaks, hickories, and maples. An interesting and important flood plain plant is the switch cane. Growing in thick canebrakes, its leaves, tips, and underground stems are savored by local wildlife. In terms of edible leaf production, it is thought to be one of the most productive plants on earth.

Alluvial rivers play an important role in coastal commercial and recreational fisheries. Countless hours are spent by fishermen on Georgia rivers searching for supper or that trophy bass. Georgia's most famous fish, the world's record large-mouth bass, was taken from an oxbow lake in the flood plain of the Ocmulgee River. An extensive commercial shad industry depends on rivers of coastal Georgia. Almost two-thirds of the shad production in Georgia is in the Altamaha River, which remains fairly free of impoundments and pollution. The Ogeechee and Savannah Rivers are also important shad producers. Eels are also caught here, but as most Americans have not developed a taste for them, they are shipped to Europe where they are regarded as a gourmet treat. Occasionally a sturgeon is captured and provides roe for delectable caviar.

The value of these rivers to society is just being realized. The natural filtering of the flood plain provides an efficient means of treating agricultural, industrial, and personal wastes.

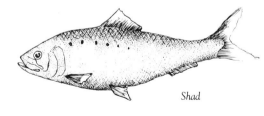

Shad

Shad yields for 1983 approached 230,000 pounds valued at $175,000.

As long as the system is not overloaded, these swamps are highly efficient water treatment systems. Obviously, activity which severely disrupts this ecosytem, such as channelization, impoundment, or extensive timber clearing, will alter this process. Such long-term consequences must be taken into account and balanced against the short-term gains.

The great river swamps offer a rich haven for wildlife. Such swamps were the last refuge of the now-extinct Carolina parakeet and ivory-billed woodpecker. They are still the preferred home of the barred owl and the Mississippi and swallow-tailed kites. The staccato call of the pileated woodpecker is heard here frequently. The strikingly beautiful prothonotary warbler also is found in these swamps. Wild turkeys are common, and the spectacular wood duck nests in hollows of giant trees. Alligators, turtles, and snakes are numerous near the waterways. Otter, mink, and beaver are found in and near the water. Deer, raccoon, opossum, bobcats, and an occasional black bear also inhabit the bottomland forest.

As human populations increase, upland areas are increasingly urbanized or converted into agricultural lands. Much of the existing woodland is now utilized in the monoculture of pine. Diversity of the bottomland hardwood forests of the alluvial river swamps stand in refreshing contrast to these comparatively sterile environments. The river swamp green belts have incalculable value as an educational and recreational resource. Ironically, in colonial times the large rivers were the lifeblood of Georgia, because they served as the highways of human travel and commerce. Today, these rivers and flood plains remain as natural corridors of life in our drastically altered landscape.

Tidewater Rivers

Interstate 95 provides a good introduction to the tidal river environment, particularly as it crosses the Jerico and Medway rivers. Good places to examine rivers under tidal influence include the Savannah National Wildlife Refuge, the Altamaha River Waterfowl Area, and Crooked River State Park.

Tidewater rivers are those whose flow is significantly influenced by the rise and fall of the tides. Actually, there are two different types of tidewater rivers. The first type is short and, except

Osprey

for periods of heavy rain, carries only estuarine waters of varying degrees of salinity. The second type is a short segment of a larger river as it encounters tidal ebb and flow. With the exception of the Canoochee and Ebenezer, all of coastal Georgia's alluvial and blackwater rivers have a stretch which is tidally-influenced.

Tidewater rivers are generally very wide and are bordered by a sequence of fresh, brackish, and salt marshes as these rivers flow to the ocean. It was in the upper reaches of tidewater rivers that the great rice plantations of the 18th and 19th centuries flourished.

The original swamp forest, primarily bald cypress and tupelo, was cleared for the large agricultural fields. A series of dikes, canals, and locks was constructed. By taking advantage of tidal fluctuations, the fields could be alternately flooded and drained. The remains of these old rice fields can be seen as one crosses the flood plains of the upper portions of the Savannah and Altamaha River deltas. In some areas the dikes have been maintained over the years, and the fields are flooded periodically for migrating waterfowl. The forested portion of the tidal flood plain is still dominated by bald cypress and tupelo. Closer to the ocean, the salinity of the water increases. Consequently, trees thin out and give way to extensive brackish and saltwater marshes.

The river marshes, especially these old rice fields, offer spectacular opportunities to view waterfowl. Numerous rails and gallinules breed here. The prehistoric appearing anhinga, or snakebird, is a year round resident. It swims with only head and neck above water much like a snake, then disappears to spear a fish underwater with its bayonet-like beak. Because of a lack of oil in its feathers, the anhinga must spread its wings in the sunlight to dry before flying. Thus, it is often seen perched over the water with wings outstretched.

Wading birds are also plentiful. The sedate great blue heron is frequently seen patiently awaiting fish, frogs, snakes, or a baby alligator along the banks. Slightly smaller in size is the stately great egret. This pure white bird is a common sight. The smaller snowy egret, tri-colored (formerly Louisiana) heron, little blue heron, and green heron also abound.

These marshes and impoundments are favored wintering grounds for ducks and occasionally geese. Pintails, mallards, shovelers, teal, scaup, and ringneck are common.

The dead or dying trees at the edge of the river or marsh are common nesting sites for the osprey (fish hawk). With a wing span of nearly six feet, this expert fisherman can be seen soaring over open waters searching for food. Plunging from heights up to 100 or 150 feet, the bird strikes the water feet first, and usually emerges with an enviable prize clutched in its talons. After a midair pause to shake the feathers, the osprey ascends to a favorite perch to eat its catch.

The river marsh and old rice fields are also hunting grounds for the bald eagle. Quite uncommon in Georgia, its population may be on the increase in the southland. Populations of the eagle, as well as the osprey, reached a low during the 1960's as a result of the widespread use of chlorinated hydrocarbon pesticides such as DDT. These chemicals break down slowly, and once ingested, tend to accumulate in animal tissues. Each succeeding organism in the food chain builds up higher and higher levels of toxic products. Large birds at the end of the food chain, such as the pelicans and eagles, are particularly vulnerable to these pesticides. It is believed that this causes a bird's eggshell to be thinned, which severely limits their reproductive capabilities.

Since the banning of certain pesticides in this country, the decline in reproduction may have been reversed. The population seems to be on the upswing. Indiscriminate and malicious shooting by the uninformed public remains a major threat to the endangered eagle. Lead poisoning from ingesting lead pellets in wounded waterfowl and relentless destruction of their critical habitat also pose a threat.

Bald Eagle

Winter and early spring in the Savannah National Wildlife Refuge offer the best opportunity to view the bald eagle.

SWAMPS

The best swamp the visitor may see is the Okefenokee Swamp. Entrances include Stephen Foster State Park, the Suwannee Canal Recreation Area, and the Okefenokee Swamp Park.

The term swamp in this section refers to a depressed freshwater wetland that is generally forested. Water flow may be slow, but significant. These swamps can be classified according to their geological makeup and their predominant vegetation. Swamps support hardwood forests

41

consisting of slow-growing bald cypress with an understory of tupelo. The cypress has a wide buttressed base and "knees" which protrude from the dark waters. These "knees" are thought to provide aeration for the often submerged root system of the cypress. Sadly, such stands of massive timber are rare today. The temptation exists to fill in swamps and grow pine trees; however, endangered and threatened plant species also share these wetlands.

Cypress and tupelo ponds are shallow depressions which generally occur in pine flatlands. They range in size from less than an acre to several acres. Cypress ponds are particularly subject to significant fluctuations in water level and often experience a dry phase during the year. This dry phase makes these ponds susceptible to periodic fires, which prevent a thick peat layer from accumulating.

Semi-aquatic environments play an important role in the life of the surrounding uplands. They are teeming with animal life and are seasonal breeding areas for numerous species of frogs, toads, and salamanders. Larger ponds are important nesting sites and feeding areas for water-fowl. These ponds also play a role in maintaining the water table, functioning as reservoirs to hold excess rainwater. They also serve as natural water treatment sites, holding runoff water and removing many pollutants in surface water.

Unfortunately, the vital role of these wetlands to local wildlife and their importance in maintaining clear water are not widely appreciated. They are all too often cleared and drained to support crops of pine.

The bay swamp, or bayhead, is an uncommon wetland environment found in coastal Georgia. It is a wet, luxuriant, evergreen forest. A high water table with little standing water produces these peat-filled forests. Most striking is the dominance of sweetbay, myrtle, and redbay trees. These unique environments are found at the heads of streams, in sandhill depressions, and at the edge of the alluvial flood plains.

Savannas and herb bogs are wet grassland communities which depend on periodic fires to maintain themselves. A variety of bald cypress and pond pine may be found here. It is, however, the character of the herbaceous plants which make these areas unique.

Here one finds an array of wildflowers and carnivorous plants unmatched in coastal Georgia. Meadow beauty, hatpins, terrestrial orchids, and lilies are common. However, the flowery profusion belies the underlying acidic, nutrient-poor soil. One way in which plants have adapted to this environment has been to supplement nutrient intake with a diet of insects. The carnivorous pitcher plants often grow in profusion here. Their erect trumpets are hollow and lined with tiny downward-pointing hairs. Unsuspecting insects are trapped inside, unable to escape. They add to the plant's nourishment by dying in a pool inside of the plant's leaves and by being slowly dissolved. These environments, because they are continually falling victim to grazing, draining, and plant collecting, are becoming increasingly rare. Pitcher plants are endangered in Georgia and are protected by state law.

Carolina bays are unique to the Southeastern Coastal Plain. Found from northern Florida to southern Virginia, they are elliptical depressions of several hundred feet to several miles across. They are oriented along a southeast-northwest axis, and usually have an elevated sandy ridge at the southeast rim. Their origin is subject to debate. They are thought to be the result of an ancient meteor shower or the scouring action of prehistoric winds. Carolina bays contain a variety of wetland communities. In the deeper portions, open water and cypress may be found. Shrub bay and typical swamp vegetation may be located further in the interior.

Perhaps the most famous American swamp is the Okefenokee. It is 423,721 acres of wetland found in the southeastern corner of Georgia. An ancient barrier island shoreline, Trail Ridge, forms the eastern boundary of the swamp. A large, peat-filled shallow lake has formed behind it with dark, acidic water.

Within the Okefenokee are found a variety of different wetland habitats. Cypress bays are forests of cypress, tupelo and bay trees anchored in the thick peat. Between the cypress bays and prairies one finds sphagnum bogs which contain fewer trees and a thick mat of herbaceous plants. There are large expanses of prairie which are shallow vegetation-filled ponds without trees. Open water is unusual, confined to a few narrow lakes and prairie rivers.

Pickerel Weed

43

Further natural and human history of the Okefenokee is given later in this book. Almost the entire swamp, along with 9,000 acres of surrounding uplands, are included within the Okefenokee National Wildlife Refuge. It is one of the few large wilderness forests which persists in this portion of our country. It has immense value for recreation and scientific research.

Such natural areas have an immeasurable, intangible worth to our society which is yet to be appreciated. Their unspoiled beauty provides solace to the sagging human spirit and may provide refuge for generations to come.

DRIVING TOURS

Mainland
Upland Habitat

THE BARTRAM TRAIL

The Bartram Trail Conference
Mr. Elliott Edwards
431 East 63rd Street
Savannah, GA 31405

William Bartram, America's first native-born naturalist, spent many years of his life traveling through what are now the Southeastern states in the late 1700's, studying and collecting specimens of native flora and fauna. Today the Bartram Trail attempts to retrace his footsteps through coastal Georgia.

William Bartram first arrived in Georgia in 1765 with his father, John Bartram, who was the Royal Botanist for King George III of England. Their purpose was to collect horticultural specimens suitable for botanical gardens in Europe and in colonial America. One of the discoveries made by the Bartrams was of a beautiful flowering tree, subsequently named *Franklinia alatamaha* after John Bartram's friend, Benjamin Franklin, and the Altamaha River. The tree was last seen in the wild in 1803, but the specimens collected by the Bartrams in 1765 were successfully propagated and serve as the original source for all the *Franklinias* that exist today.

William Bartram returned to Georgia in 1773, and traveled through much of the Southeast until 1777. Returning to Philadelphia, William expanded his field notes and published the results in 1791, as <u>Travels Through North & South Carolina, Georgia, East & West Florida, The Cherokee Country, The Extensive Terretories of The Muscogulges, or Creek Confederacy, And The Country of The Choctaws</u>. Bartram's <u>Travels</u> represents one of the earliest and most detailed descriptions of the Southeastern environment. As such, it was immediately hailed in Europe by both the scientific and literary communities. Bartram's <u>Travels</u>, available in several different editions, is an excellent companion for anyone wishing to retrace his route.

Most of the Bartrams' routes through the Southeast have been traced by Bartram Trail members. Following the routes provides a fascinating way to explore the region's early natural

Driving Tour Directions
Trail Sections of the Savannah River Road, Chatham and Effingham Counties
For a relaxed one-day drive, exit from I-95 at exit #19 and proceed north on GA Hwy. 21 to Rincon. At the overpass and 4th Street (Rincon-Stillwell Road #307) turn right. Go 5.7 miles to the intersection with GA Hwy. 275. Turn right and go 3 miles to New Ebenezer (see page 78). Return 3 miles to #307 (Rincon-Stillwell Road) and turn right. After approximately 1 mile note Ebenezer Creek (see page 174). Continue 1.5 miles to Stillwell and turn right onto Stillwell-Clyo Road (#308). Proceed 9.5 miles to Clyo and turn left onto 4th Street, right onto Marion Road, left onto Clyo-Kildare Road, then right onto GA Hwy. 119. Proceed 2.8 miles north to the entrance of Tuckassee King Landing (see page 89).

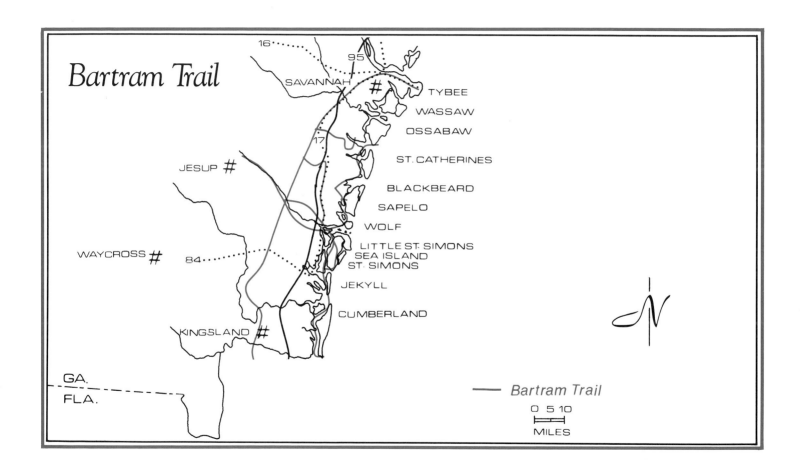

Bartram Trail

16
95
SAVANNAH
TYBEE
WASSAW
OSSABAW
17
ST. CATHERINES
JESUP #
BLACKBEARD
SAPELO
WOLF
LITTLE ST. SIMONS
SEA ISLAND
WAYCROSS #
84
ST. SIMONS
JEKYLL
CUMBERLAND
KINGSLAND #

GA.
FLA.

—— Bartram Trail

0 5 10
MILES

N

48

and social history. Many of the routes followed by the Bartrams were either trails established by the Indians or roads constructed by the colonists.

As both of these often became the bases for roads in the twentieth century, it is possible to follow much of the Bartrams travels by automobile. Some of the Bartram Trail has been marked in coastal Georgia. A conference goal is to locate and mark the entire route of William Bartram.

When William Bartram departed from Savannah in April, 1773, he visited a number of sites that are described in this guide. He traveled by horseback to Sunbury, using a route that approximated the present U.S. Highway 17, and then to Colonel's Island (erroneously called St. Catherines in the Travels) where he observed Indian shell mounds and a great variety of tree, shrubs, and herbaceous plants. He also recorded a number of animals, including the eagle and osprey, and some that can only be observed in captivity — the wolf, the bear, and "tyger" or panther.

Returning to Midway, Bartram turned south again and traveled "the high road" to Fort Barrington on the Altamaha River. He passed by the LeConte-Woodmanston Plantation, one of the large rice plantations in the region. South of the plantation, he left the main road to Fort Barrington and headed for Darien. The intervening swamps and creeks confused Bartram, and eventually he lost his way. He was finally taken in by Lachlan McIntosh and given shelter for several days. He then proceeded to Fort Barrington, very likely following what is now the road to Cox, and then on what is described in this guide as the road to Fort Barrington. Somewhere along this road, Bartram found two beautiful shrubs, one of which was the *Franklinia alatamaha* that he and his father had discovered twelve years earlier. Modern researchers have attempted to locate living examples of the tree in this area, but many days of searching have been to no avail. The other shrub discovered by the Bartrams was the Georgia fever tree, a striking shrub still seen today along creek banks.

Having obtained specimens and seeds of some curious plants, Bartram returned to Savannah. He was then invited by the Superintendent of Indian Affairs to go to Augusta for a Congress and Treaty with the Creek Indians.

Driving Trail Directions: Trail Sections in Coastal Corridor, Chatham, Bryan, Liberty and McIntosh Counties.
Begin at the Savannah Visitors' Center on West Broad Street in downtown Savannah. Proceed south on West Broad Street to Anderson Street. Turn right onto Anderson Street. At the stop sign turn left onto Great Ogeechee Rd. (U.S. Hwy. 17). Follow Hwy. 17 to the Ogeechee River and Kings' Ferry Park (boat ramp and swimming area). After crossing the Ogeechee River, continue south through Bryan County into Liberty County. As you approach GA. Hwy. 38, observe the Midway Museum and church (see page 125). Turn left just beyond the church onto Old Sunbury Rd. noting the historic markers. Continue east about 7.8 miles. Turn left on County Road 15 and proceed 2.8 miles to Fort Morris and Sunbury Historic Site (see page 133). After exiting Sunbury onto paved road, turn right and proceed 0.2 miles to the end of the pavement noting Sunbury historic markers. Travel back the same road and return to Hwy. 38. Continue left on Hwy. 38 to its end and loop around Colonels Island via County Road 1. Return to Midway. From Midway south the Bartrams' two routes follow U.S. Hwy. 17 to Darien and GA. Hwy. 25 towards Fort Barrington (see page 110). An alternate route can be taken to LeConte-Woodmanston Plantation (see page 121).

From Savannah, Bartram then traveled towards Augusta, probably following part of what is now GA Route 21, the Old Augusta Road. On May 5, 1773, he stopped at Ebenezer near the banks of the Savannah River. After visiting Augusta and participating in a survey west of there, Bartram returned to Savannah. He then proceeded again to Darien and the Altamaha River.

Continued explorations of the Georgia coast took Bartram to Broughton Island (now part of the Altamaha River Waterfowl Area) and Fort Frederica on St. Simons Island. He was a beachcomber on St. Simons, delighting in the variety of shellfish washed up on the beach. Embarking at Frederica for East Florida, Bartram sailed past Jekyll Island and Cumberland. Threatened by Indian raiders, the boat returned to Frederica, but Bartram was let ashore on Cumberland Island.

Bartram also visited Sapelo Island, but the date of his visit is uncertain. On Sapelo Bartram encountered a rattlesnake whose spiral coil formed a mound half the height of his knees. But since the rattlesnake left Bartram and his companions alone, they in turn did the same.

It was probably in the summer of 1776 that William Bartram retraced an old Indian trail and Post Road which he and his father earlier took from the Fort Barrington ferry on the Altamaha to King's Ferry, Florida on the St. Mary's River. His Travels give us an early account of the nearby Okefenokee Swamp.

Much of the route traveled by William Bartram has been compromised by modern developments, and only a few scattered segments retain the natural characteristics that Bartram saw in 1773-1776. However, these roads still traverse some of the most scenic areas of Georgia, and this tour allows the visitor to get a sense of life in colonial Georgia.

INTERSTATE 95

Millions of people drive through Georgia on Interstate 95 each year without understanding the landscape that they are seeing and without realizing that they are passing through fascinating natural areas and within minutes of significant natural and historical sites. This superhighway cuts across largely uninhabited land, thus frequently affording a picture of what undisturbed coastal plant communities are really like. Moreover, it sometimes veers closer to the ocean than Highway 17, permitting better views of the marsh and catching rivers and creeks at wider points.

During the colonial era, visitors to the Georgia coast traveled primarily by water using the major rivers – the Altamaha, the Savannah, or the Ogeechee – to transport items for trade. Other travelers moved along the coast in offshore sailing vessels, or through the tidal rivers behind the islands in boats or canoes. When they traveled on the mainland, travelers used the Indian trails which were on sand ridges, remnants of ancient barrier islands. Many of these trails became roads which in turn became modern highway routes. Interstate 95 is an exception to this general pattern because it was built where a roadway did not previously exist.

Some of the highlights one can see while driving along the interstate are: alluvial, blackwater and tidewater rivers; salt marsh, fresh and brackish water swamps; planted pine forest, deciduous hardwood forests, and cypress swamps; and, nesting areas for hawks, osprey, herons, and egrets. The reader may refer to the Natural Communities section of this guidebook while driving I-95 to obtain an in-depth understanding of the coastal ecosystems.

Georgia-South Carolina State Line

The medians and borders of the interstate have been left in their natural state wherever possible, which makes the trip more interesting and saves the state money on landscaping. The shoulders and ditches have been in place long enough to support a somewhat diverse flora. At different times of the summer one may see pickerel weed (purple), atamasco lily (white), pitcher plants (yellow), daisies, and a variety of other wildflowers.

Great Egret

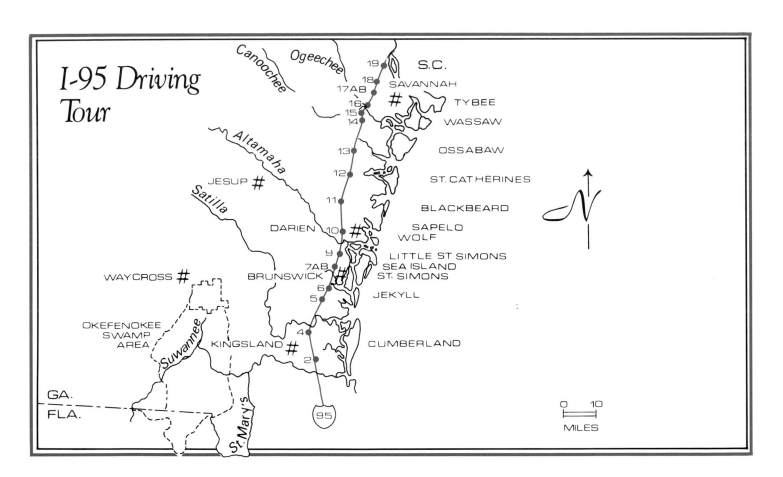

I-95 Driving Tour

Canoochee

Ogeechee

19
18
17AB
16
15
14

S.C.

SAVANNAH #

TYBEE

WASSAW

OSSABAW

13

12

11

Altamaha

ST. CATHERINES

BLACKBEARD

JESUP #

Satilla

DARIEN 10 #

SAPELO
WOLF

9

7AB

LITTLE ST SIMONS
SEA ISLAND
ST. SIMONS

WAYCROSS #

BRUNSWICK #

6

5

JEKYLL

OKEFENOKEE
SWAMP
AREA

Suwannee

KINGSLAND #

4

2

CUMBERLAND

GA.
FLA.

St. Mary's

95

0   10

MILES

N

March, April, and May will find the shoulders ablaze in color when seeded clover lays out a red carpet welcome mat for visitors. The Georgia Department of Transportation does not mow the borders of the interstate until after the clover and other wildflowers have finished blooming.

The first glimpse of Georgia is the Savannah River. This alluvial river has headwaters in the mountains of Georgia and serves as the border between Georgia and South Carolina. The Savannah River meets the Atlantic Ocean north of Tybee Island. The river has always served as a transportation route for people and goods from the upland to the sea. High bluffs and extensive swamps border the river.

Just east of the I-95 crossing is Mulberry Grove, the now abandoned site of the plantation of Revolutionary War hero General Nathanael Greene. It was at Mulberry Grove that Eli Whitney invented the cotton gin. Whitney, a tutor at Mulberry Grove, conceived of the cotton gin while spending his evenings helping to pull the seeds out of the cotton fibers. Further down stream is the historic port of Savannah. Several large industries and historic forts are located on the Savannah River.

Exit 19 - Highway 21 - Augusta Road
Highway 21, which crosses I-95 at Exit 19, became known as Augusta Road because it has been the main overland route to the interior of the state since the coast was first occupied. Its travelers have included William Bartram, a naturalist who traveled the east in the 1700's (see section on William Bartram Trail) and John Muir, a conservationist who founded the Sierra Club.

Exit 18 - U.S. 80 - Savannah
Pipemaker's Canal, which is crossed by I-95, was one of the many canals that was dug to drain the lowland. The Irene Indian Mound and the remains of a Moravian Village were excavated from a site where the canal meets the Savannah River.

Indian artifacts and an explanation of their lifestyle can be seen at the Marine Extension Center on Skidaway Island and the Savannah Science Museum.

Exit 17B - Interstate 16 - to Macon

Exit 17A - Interstate 16 - to Savannah
A mixed evergreen deciduous forest with interspersed wetlands borders this stretch. This particular forest is an example of the natural succession of a forest which begins with small grasses, small shrubs, and moves to large shrubs, pine, and finally oak, magnolia, and hickory. These woods burned in the 1950's. They have reforested themselves in the typical manner of succeeding species dominating the predecessor. This forest, if left undisturbed by fire and man, will become a hardwood forest by the middle of the 21st century.

Exit 16 - Highway 204 - Savannah
The first indication that one is approaching the Ogeechee River is the causeway crossing the river swamp. Just west of the bridge the Canoochee joins the Ogeechee River. The Canoochee River, a blackwater stream, flows through Fort Stewart, the home of the 24th Infantry Division, part of the nation's Rapid Deployment Force.

The Ogeechee, an alluvial river with headwaters in the piedmont of Georgia, was recently studied for possible inclusion in the National Wild and Scenic River System. The National Park Service, which conducted the study, found the river eligible for inclusion because of its outstanding beauty and recreational opportunities. Because only a few people and organizations were in favor of gaining protection for the river, the river remains unprotected from future development. The Nature Conservancy and The Georgia Conservancy are seeking to preserve the beauty of the river through conservation easements.

The river is easily accessible, with many ramps, and is very popular for fishing and boating. Ogeechee River shad are popular with sport fishermen, as well as being a profitable commercial fish. The roe from the female shad are shipped throughout the country.

Exit 15 - Fort Stewart and Richmond Hill
In this stretch, one will see intermittent pasture land. Often, cattle are grazing with an accompanying cattle egret. The cattle egret is an old-world bird which arrived in Georgia from

Africa around 1950. It was introduced to North America without man's help, and presents no known filth or disease problems, such as starlings and pigeons do. It has rapidly extended its range along the coast and inland. Like other herons it breeds in rookeries. Cattle egrets are white with yellow bills, crests and legs. They are seen in flocks or singly in pastures feeding on insects. They often perch on cattle and use them to flush insects from the grasses. At dusk flocks of them may be observed heading back to the rookeries.

There is, of course, much bird life along the interstate. Several kinds of large dark birds either perched or flying are sure to be seen. The smallest of these, the common crow, can be told by its flapping flight and somewhat pointed wings. The black and turkey vultures, which soar and circle, are recognized by the upward "V" of their wings. The red-tailed hawk is also common, although not as numerous as the crow or vulture. It soars on stubbier, flatter wings, and is lighter than the vulture – one may even glimpse its reddish tail. In the heavily forested areas a large pileated woodpecker occasionally darts across the highway at treetop level. Over the marshes in winter a male marsh hawk might be noticed with a spot of white on the tail.

Southern Pine Cone

Exit 14 - Richmond Hill

By now the visitor will be aware that Georgia's coast is indeed pine country. Pine, a native species, has always been an important factor in the regional economy. Colonists used longleaf and slash pine to build houses. Nineteenth century residences were built with lovely heart-of-pine flooring. Lumber mills were a major factor in the South's economic recovery after the Civil War, and the area's move into the industrial era came in the thirties with the arrival of the pulp and paper mills. Interstate 95 offers the traveler an overview of all stages of tree farming, which primarily cultivates the southern pine. The cultivation of pine seen from I-95 is predominantly slash pine, noted for its quick growth, and mostly used for the production of paper.

North of the Jerico River, a tidewater river, needlerush marsh can be seen with spartina growing along the water's edge. The spartina (or cordgrass) is green in spring and summer, golden in the fall and winter, and always breathtaking. To the west the marsh has been filled for real estate development. This took place before the value of the marsh was realized. Georgia was one of the first states to acknowledge the many contributions made by the wetlands to man and nature and subsequently to protect them. Scientists estimate an acre of salt marsh is worth at least $20,000. That estimate does not include the aesthetic value of the marsh, which may be its greatest value.

To the east the salt marsh stretches to the horizon. The marshes that one passes on this section of the highway are the upper reaches of St. Catherines Sound. On the southeastern side of the river, there is a "spoil" area created by the disposal of material dredged during the process of highway construction. Red-tailed and red-shouldered hawks might be seen in this area.

Exit 13 - Midway and Sunbury (U.S. 32 and GA. 38)
Visitors driving through this area will see the pine tree farms which are established on higher well-drained soil. Periodically, the visitor will note lowlands associated with small creeks and swamps. These areas are not suitable for pine culture because pine trees require better drainage to thrive. In these lowlands native hardwoods and swamp forests are allowed to grow.

The North Newport River is a tidewater river with abundant needlerush marsh. The water is more brackish than most estuarine tidewaters.

To the west, approaching exit #12, notice the pulp mill. There are five paper mills on Georgia's coast. These mills are built close to a source of raw material. One of the by-products of a mill's operation is the sulfurous odor, which is occasionally apparent to the visitor.

Exit 12 - Newport
Bulltown Swamp adjoins South Newport River which forms the Liberty County/McIntosh County border. This swamp is also part of the water course of the LeConte-Woodmanston Plantation, which is currently being renovated by the Garden Club of Georgia. Naturally fluctuating water levels of the swamps were utilized by 18th and 19th century planters in their cultivation of rice.

The forest on the central Georgia coast in this area consists of planted pines, acid flatwoods, and blueberry bushes that can tolerate the high acidity of the soil. Armadillos, a medium-sized

Peregrine Falcon

mammal, are now abundant in the region, having migrated from Central America via Florida and into Georgia over the last 50 years. The saw palmetto is noticeable in the underbrush as one progresses southward.

A large cypress on the east side marks Buckhill Swamp. When crossing the swamp, several bald cypress trees can be seen. The bald cypress is known as a tree of poorly drained soils and of freshwater swamps where it obtains sunlight by thrusting its crown high above other species. A deciduous conifer, it is one of the oldest forms of tree vegetation existing today. Nature has endowed it with a resinous protection that has enabled the species to withstand attacks of insects and disease. Rare virgin stands are 400-600 years old. Local Indians used the soft, strong, durable logs to fabricate canoes, called "dugouts." The white man used the wood for small boats, docks, building siding, shingles, and for many other purposes where lasting qualities were desired. Bald cypress is extremely difficult to harvest and has become rare because of the great demand and damage to its habitats.

Exit 11 - Townsend and Eulonia, (GA. 99)
Just south of exit #11 there is another stand of bald cypress in a flood plain known as Young's Swamp. Here also is another pine plantation. Pine, a renewable resource, is managed on a thirty year rotation. These trees which are planted to harvest are contantly thinned, each cutting being sold commercially until the ultimate clear cutting, when the field is totally cleared of trees and prepared for replanting. On the east side of the highway several lone bald cypress trees mark Kings Swamp.

The edge and median have native loblolly pine, sweet gum, red maple, willow oak, laurel oak, water oak, tupelo, inkberry, huckleberry, and saw palmetto. Azaleas and oleander have been planted in the open areas.

Exit 10 - Darien
At this point, the picturesque Altamaha, an alluvial river, is in the delta form, split into four different rivers and a creek. The river swamp here differs from what one sees crossing the Ogeechee and the Savannah river swamps in that the Altamaha delta is a transition area

Bald Cypress

57

where the saltwater from the ocean and sound are meeting the freshwater from the interior. The trees have given way to grasses and shrubs that can tolerate the influx of salty water. Magnificent stands of bald cypress are evident upriver throughout this delta.

As one crosses the Darien River, a keen eye may spot an osprey nest built high in old cypress trees. These nests are quite large and with some luck one may also see an osprey soaring nearby.

This portion of the Altamaha River was used in the 19th century for the cultivation of rice. Some of the old rice fields are managed today to attract migratory waterfowl, and during the winter months ducks can be seen feeding in the Altamaha delta. The Altamaha River Waterfowl Area is bisected by I-95.

Historically, the Altamaha has served as a dividing line, first between the Spanish and the Indians, and later, after the Battle of Bloody Marsh (when the Spanish were convinced to give up any thoughts of possessing Georgia), as a dividing line between the Indians to the south and the British colonists to the north. Initial plans have been prepared for an Altamaha River Park, which would protect the river in its natural state and provide boat launching ramps, hiking trails, and campsites for public use.

White-tailed Deer

Exit 9 - GA. Highway 99
The versatility of the pine tree is the reason for its success commercially. Early explorers discovered the usefulness of pine for its sap, with which they caulked boats and coated the riggings of sailing ships to prevent rotting. Thus, the business of producing chemicals from the pine sap became known as naval stores.

Exit 8 - Golden Isles Parkway
Driving south, a quick detour off the interstate onto the exit ramp returning to I-95 will reveal a small bald cypress and bay swamp.

Exit 7 and 7A - Brunswick and Jesup
On the western side of this interchange there is a tall brick chimney, marking the site of a

World War I munitions factory. The armistice was signed before the factory was completed and production of munitions was never begun.

When approaching Gibson Creek, the visitor will cross the marshes of Glynn County, made famous as the source of inspiration to Sidney Lanier's poem "Marshes of Glynn." This broad expanse of marsh is a coastal Georgia trademark, for its beauty and value are difficult to rival. In the marsh approaching Turtle River there are scrawny trees known as tamarisk trees. These Mediterranean plants were introduced to Georgia as seed in the ballast of sailing ships during the 19th century. The Turtle and South Brunswick rivers are tidewater estuaries which empty into St. Simons Sound. Between these rivers is Blythe Island. On the pine forests of Blythe Island a young cypress forest is beginning to establish itself on the western edge of the highway. The industry visible to the east is a paper mill and a power plant is to the west.

Exit 6 - U.S. 84
Driving along the southern coast, the visitor may have noticed several small ponds or borrow pits, where the dirt has been "borrowed" to fill in low areas of the roadbed. The water in the pits comes from rainfall. A succession of plant growth occurs on their banks. Another of these borrow pits is just to the east before reaching the Little Satilla River. The Little Satilla River is a tidewater river.

Exit 5 - Dover Bluff
Throughout this area the visitor sees almost constant pine woodlands in varying stages of maturity. These are broken from time to time by low areas of hardwoods and more varied flora. Here the interstate skirts the upper reaches of St. Andrews Sound of which White Oak Creek is a part. Much of the view of the marsh is obstructed by a dense growth of wax myrtle shrub in the filled land next to the highway. This provides a good nesting place for the painted bunting.

At Canoe Swamp a "skeleton" forest of dead cypress trees stand as a lonely reminder of man's intervention. A natural cypress swamp is dependent on fluctuating water levels. The building of I-95 altered the drainage patterns of this swamp and subsequently killed these stately cypress.

The Satilla River is a blackwater river. Legislation has been introduced proposing this river for study for inclusion in the National Wild and Scenic River System.

Exit 4 - Woodbine

This seven mile stretch between exits #4 and #3 is almost completely wooded. The forest is more varied here compared to the intensively managed pine plantations. Bald cypress and tupelo are common, indicating lower areas. Magnolia, sweet gum, hickory, maple, and other hardwoods are more common in the upland areas. A number of larger live oak trees still remain reaching above the understory. Many of their branches are covered with the lovely resurrection fern, which transforms from its withered brown state to a luxurious green with every rainfall.

Exit 3 - Harriett's Bluff

The Crooked River just north of exit #2 is a tidal river, and the accompanying salt marsh is bordered by red cedar trees. Many of these trees are dead or dying because of frequent inundation by saltwater. The rise in the sea level has increased the amount of saltwater flowing into this arm of the sea.

Exit 2A - Colrain, Kings Bay

North of St. Marys the pine trees face some competition in their importance to the local economy. The Navy is constructing the Kings Bay Submarine Base which will support Trident nuclear submarines. The growth stimulated by this base will dramatically alter the scenery of this area in the next decade, and it will have a major economic impact on Camden County.

Exit 2 - St. Marys and Folkston

At times there are many timber areas filled with branches and rubble that seem to have been forgotten by the timber companies. Pine tree harvesting is often done by clear cutting entire fields. Bulldozers then make "wind-rows" out of branches and stumps. Later, the rotten wood is burned. Sometimes mature trees are left to reseed the fields. Other times, pine seedlings from nurseries are used to replant the fields.

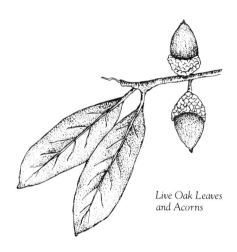

Live Oak Leaves and Acorns

Exit 1 - St. Marys Road

The east side of the interchange of exit #1 to St. Marys Road cuts through an interesting lowland area of small cypress and bay.

Georgia-Florida State Line

Entering or leaving Florida, the visitor crosses the St. Marys River, a blackwater river with headwaters in the Okefenokee Swamp. A quick summary of coastal Georgia is captured in this view of salt marsh, forest, and a tidal river.

The coast of Georgia is developing quickly, but fortunately the value of Georgia's natural bounty is recognized by a growing number of Georgia citizens.

EXCURSIONS OFF INTERSTATE 95

This section is offered to give the visitor an option of touring those sites which are most conveniently reached from Interstate 95, with site reference numbers noted in parentheses. The guide is presented in north to south driving sequence, beginning at the South Carolina state line and ending at the Florida state line. In addition, there are several alternative driving routes along I-95 which offer a nice break from the monotony of an interstate highway and involve little added travel time. These paragraphs highlight some of the exciting opportunities which await the adventurous.

Exit 19 – Highway 21 – Augusta Road
This first exit south of the Savannah River provides access to the sites west of I-95 and upstream on the Savannah River. **New Ebenezer (6)**, a community settled by Salzburgers in 1734, is approximately a thirty-minute drive from I-95. New Ebenezer's museum and historic church are near Ebenezer Creek, a backwater creek surrounded by bald cypress trees, which flows slowly into the Savannah River. **Tuckassee King Landing (13)**, a high mesic bluff overlooking the Savannah River, can also be reached from exit 19.

Exit 17A – Interstate 16 to Savannah
A ten-minute trip east of I-95 takes the traveler to Savannah. Founded in 1733, this city is today known internationally for its success in preservation of historic architecture. A visitors center located near the termination of I-16 is open year-round from 9:00 a.m. to 5:00 p.m., and is a convenient point for an orientation to this charming area. An excellent introductory film is shown there, and tours of the city leave at close intervals thoughout the day.

While all of exits 19 through 16 provide access to Savannah, the simplest route for the visitor is I-16 at exit 17A. Savannah is convenient to a number of the most accessible historic and ecological sites on the northern coast, including the following:

• **Bonaventure Cemetery (1)** – visited by John Muir

Monarch Butterfly on Milkweed

- **Fort Jackson (2)** — with an interpretive program
- **Fort Pulaski National Monument (4)** — an "invincible" fort made obsolete by technology
- **Marine Extension Center (5)** — a saltwater aquarium
- **Oatland Island Education Center (7)** — an environmental education center
- **Savannah National Wildlife Refuge (9)** — the home of native birds and reptiles
- **Savannah Science Museum (10)** — a science, technology, and natural history museum
- **Skidaway Island State Park (12)** — an excellent camping site
- **Tybee Island (14)** — a convenient beach with many facilities
- **Wormsloe Historic Site (18)** — tabby ruins of an early settlement

For the visitor without time constraints, Savannah is also a convenient point from which to make the necessary arrangements to visit **Wassaw National Wildlife Refuge (16),** or other less accessible sites.

Exit 16 — Highway 204 — Savannah
For the northbound traveler, exit 16 is the shortest route to the **Marine Extension Center (5), Savannah Science Museum (10), Skidaway Island State Park (12),** and **Wormsloe Historic Site (18).**

Exit 15 — Fort Stewart and Richmond Hill
Just 10.5 miles east of exit 15 is the unusual combination of a Civil War earthworks fort adjacent to a state park which provides campsites and picnic areas overlooking the marshlands. **Fort McAllister (3)** along with Richmond Hill State Park is an excellent rest stop for weary travelers. The ample picnic grounds and play areas provide families with a place for rest and refreshments along with a history lesson. This is an excellent place to let children burn up energy that has accumulated from a long car ride.

Exit 14 — Richmond Hill
LeConte-Woodmanston Plantation (26), an historic site and former botanical garden, is approximately 10 miles from I-95. The Garden Club of Georgia is currently in the first steps

of recreating the formal grounds of this plantation. Southbound travelers headed for the western entrance of **Okefenokee Swamp (39)** or **Stephen C. Foster State Park (39b)** can exit here for a more scenic route to the swamp.

Exit 13 – Midway and Sunbury (U.S. 32 and GA. Highway 38)
To the west of I-95 is **Midway (28).** The church, with a simple, stark design, suggests the congregation's New England origin. The museum and oak-shaded cemetery share the history of the almost forgotten community which fostered a number of the country's early leaders, including two signers of the Declaration of Independence.

To the east is **Sunbury Historic Site (31)**, which includes a museum and remains of an earthworks fort. Sunbury was once Georgia's second busiest port, but was abandoned in 1825. This site provides a delightful place to stretch tired legs and enjoy a picnic under the pine and oak trees overlooking the marsh.

Exit 12 – Newport
Fifteen miles east of I-95 is the **Harris Neck National Wildlife Refuge (24)**. The refuge is an incredible bird sanctuary that was the site of an airfield during World War II.

For the southbound traveler weary of interstate travel, this exit is one of several which allow one to leave the interstate and take U.S. Highway 17 for a distance of from 10 to 46 miles without incurring much additional time. Travel will be along a two-lane highway, occasionally canopied with magnificent oaks. The return to I-95 can be easily made at exits 9, 10, 11, or by staying on Highway 17 through Brunswick to exit 6.

For the northbound traveler, this is also the most convenient exit to reach **LeConte-Woodmanston Plantation (26)**.

Exit 11 – Townsend and Eulonia (GA. Hwy. 99)
East of I-95 on Highway 99 are several hamlets such as Ridgeville that for generations have been fishing villages and sites for summer homes. Here lies the heart of unmodernized coastal

Great Horned Owl

Georgia. A little extra time spent wandering unpaved roads leading from Highway 99 will allow many discoveries. Highway 99 crosses U.S. Highway 17 and I-95 at this exit, and returns to Highway 17 at Darien.

Exit 10 — Darien

At an earlier time, the Altamaha River was in its own way the equivalent of Interstate 95 with extensive riverboat and timber-raft traffic. This river was a major source of timber to the port of Darien, where sailing ships bound for Europe and New England were loaded. **Fort King George (22),** built by the British to protect their southern areas from the French and Spanish, is located near the mouth of the Altamaha. On the south side of the river lies the **Hofwyl-Broadfield Plantation (25),** one of the many places along the Georgia and South Carolina coast where rice was cultivated in the 1800's. Marshlands were diked, and gates were used to flood the fields with the tide water from the rivers. Cultivation and harvesting depended upon manual labor much like cotton plantations and indigo culture.

This seven-mile section of Highway 17 between exits 9 and 10 offers a concentration of historic sites overlooking the marsh and may be one of the most convenient side trips for the I-95 traveler. The Hofwyl-Broadfield Plantation and Fort King George are two of the better interpreted sites in the central part of the Georgia coast.

In addition to these two sites, other areas of ecological significance are the **Altamaha River Waterfowl Area (19),** which almost surrounds Darien, and **the road to Fort Barrington (21),** which can be reached in about twenty minutes from I-95.

The McIntosh County Welcome Center is open Monday through Friday from 8:30 a.m. to 5:00 p.m., and on Saturday until 1:00 p.m. Reservations and ticket purchases for the **Sapelo Island (30)** ferry must be made here. The traveler with a more flexible time schedule may also want to obtain information on access to **Blackbeard Island National Wildlife Refuge (20)** and **Wolf Island National Wildlife Refuge (32).**

Cabbage Palm

Exit 9 — GA Highway 99
This exit on the south side of the Altamaha River allows an efficient return to I-95 for the northbound visitor to the sites identified under exit 10.

Traveling north, the visitor can exit east to U.S. Highway 17, visit **Hofwyl-Broadfield Plantation (25)** and **Fort King George (22)**, and return to I-95 at exit 10; or continue on Highway 17 until it crosses I-95 at exit 12.

Exit 8 — Golden Isles Parkway
The Golden Isles Parkway provides convenient access to a number of sites located on or near several islands east of Brunswick, which include:

- **Jekyll Island (35)** — an affordable resort and beach community
- **Overlook Park & DNR Exhibit Room (36)** — a mainland site overlooking the marshes of Glynn
- **St. Simons Island (37)** — location of the Museum of Coastal History, Christ Church, and Fort Frederica National Monument
- **Sea Island (38)** — an interesting, but private, resort island

With advance reservations, visitors can reach the boat landing to **Little St. Simons Island (27)** from this exit.

Over the past century this area has been a vacation retreat for the wealthy. Today, it is a convenient, attractive destination for families who enjoy the beach, bicycling, camping, or a variety of other activities. The 25-minute drive from I-95 crosses the marshland which has been carefully protected by Georgians.

The Brunswick-Golden Isles Visitors Center is located on the Golden Isles Parkway near the causeway to St. Simons Island. The center is open seven days a week from 9:00 a.m. to 5:00 p.m., and a 13½-minute movie introduces the visitor to the Golden Isles. Old Town Brunswick, a Registered National Historic District of Victorian homes and squares, is located a few blocks west of Highway 17.

Gray Squirrel

Exit 6 – U.S. Highway 84

The **Okefenokee Swamp (39)**, a 423,721-acre blackwater swamp left by the retreating sea, is accessible from several entrances. Entrances to the north, west, and east sides of the swamp are listed in the site descriptions. From one day to a week can be spent learning about this unique place. The timing of a visit can be significant; therefore, reading the site narratives and an advance call to the Okefenokee National Wildlife Refuge is recommended.

Just over an hour from I-95 is **Laura S. Walker State Park (40)**. This park, with its lake and camping areas, offers the most convenient accommodations to **Okefenokee Swamp Park (39a)**. From this exit one can also reach **Stephen C. Foster State Park (39b)** in 2½ hours, and experience the open lakes and cypress forests of the swamp. The **Suwannee Canal Recreation Area (39c)** is best reached from exit 5 for southbound travelers, or exit 2 for northbound travelers.

The northbound visitor can use exit 6 to reach Brunswick, the Golden Isles and other sites as listed under exit 8.

Exit 2 – St. Marys and Folkston (GA. Highway 40)

Crooked River State Park (33) is approximately 10 miles from I-95, and a good rest stop for the weary traveler. **Cumberland Island National Seashore (34)** is a special place worth at least a day to anyone who values the beauty of the barrier islands. It is accessible from St. Marys where the National Park Service operates a passenger ferry. Access to Cumberland is restricted so that it will retain its primitive character; therefore, reservations for a day trip or overnight camping are essential. The site description provides information needed to make the arrangements – but the visitor may need to plan ahead during most of the year.

For northbound travelers, exit 2 provides access to the eastern entrance of Okefenokee Swamp, **Suwannee Canal Recreation Area (39c)**.

Exit 1 – St. Marys Road

This exit can be used by the northbound traveler to reach the passenger ferry for **Cumberland Island National Seashore (34)** in St. Marys.

Swamp Habitat

NORTHERN COAST

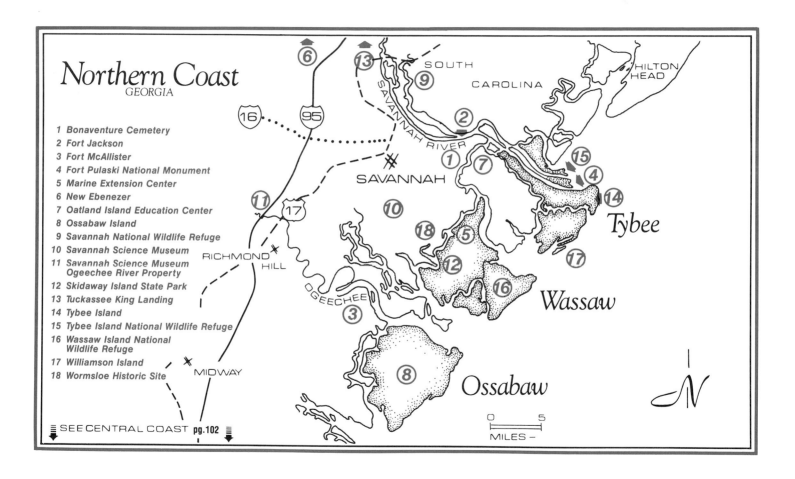

Northern Coast
GEORGIA

1 Bonaventure Cemetery
2 Fort Jackson
3 Fort McAllister
4 Fort Pulaski National Monument
5 Marine Extension Center
6 New Ebenezer
7 Oatland Island Education Center
8 Ossabaw Island
9 Savannah National Wildlife Refuge
10 Savannah Science Museum
11 Savannah Science Museum
   Ogeechee River Property
12 Skidaway Island State Park
13 Tuckassee King Landing
14 Tybee Island
15 Tybee Island National Wildlife Refuge
16 Wassaw Island National
   Wildlife Refuge
17 Williamson Island
18 Wormsloe Historic Site

SEE CENTRAL COAST pg.102

SOUTH
CAROLINA

HILTON
HEAD

SAVANNAH RIVER

SAVANNAH

Tybee

Wassaw

RICHMOND
HILL

OGEECHEE

MIDWAY

Ossabaw

0   5
MILES

N

70

BONAVENTURE CEMETERY — 1

Bonaventure Cemetery
City of Savannah
330 Bonaventure Road
Savannah, GA 31404
telephone 912/235-4227

Hours of Operation
8:00 a.m.-5:00 p.m. Monday-Friday, noon-2:00 p.m. Saturday, 2:00 p.m.-4:00 p.m. Sunday.

Directions
Exit I-95 at exit #17 for I-16. Proceed toward Savannah. Exit I-16 at the 37th Street exit #35. Turn left onto 37th Street and proceed 0.3 miles to West Broad Street. Turn right onto West Broad and travel 0.3 miles to Victory Drive. Turn left onto Victory Drive (U.S. 80) and proceed 3.6 miles to the traffic light. Turn left onto Mechanics Avenue and drive 0.1 miles to Bonaventure Road. Turn left onto Bonaventure and proceed 0.8 miles. Turn right at the stop sign and enter the cemetery through the gate.

Bonaventure Cemetery in the 19th century provided respite for one of the most important persons in America's conservation movement, John Muir. In addition, Bonaventure is quite unusual, both historically and naturally. Located on the banks of the Wilmington River, the main activity at Bonaventure is simply strolling the grounds. The area is beautifully planted with large Southern magnolias which bloom in early summer; red cedars; live oaks draped with Spanish moss; and huge azaleas which bloom in the spring.

Bonaventure was originally the 18th century plantation home of Josiah and Mary Mulryne Tattnall. They planted avenues of live oaks in the form of a monogram combining the letters M and T. Mrs. Tattnall was the first to be buried at Bonaventure in 1794. The plantation house later burned to the ground.

Shortly after Bonaventure became a cemetery in 1850, the young Scotsman John Muir, out of money and expecting funds from his brother, found refuge in this beautiful spot. Camping at Bonaventure proved to be an inexpensive 5-day interim for Muir in late September of 1867. He wrote ". . .it is one of the most impressive assemblages of animal and plant creatures I have ever met. . .never since I was allowed to walk the woods have I found so impressive a company of trees as the tillandsia-draped oaks of Bonaventure."

John Muir was in Savannah as a part of his "Thousand Mile Walk to the Gulf" which began in Louisville, Kentucky. Muir later became America's most prominent advocate of environmental preservation. he was the force behind the formation of several national parks including Yosemite, and he was one of the founders and the first president of the Sierra Club.

The visitor to Bonaventure will find the same beautiful oaks described by John Muir as well as the lingering spirits of history which characterize an old cemetery. Famous sons of Savannah, such as Noble Jones of Wormsloe, his son Dr. Noble Wymberly Jones, and Edward Telfair, are buried here. Bonaventure indeed provides a relaxing way to capture the feeling of tranquility and peacefulness of the 18th and 19th centuries.

Facilities
- *brochures*
- *demonstrations*
- *exhibits*
- *museum*
- *pets on leash only*
- *picnic area*
- *restrooms*
- *special events/programs*
- *soft drink machine*
- *visitor center*

Hours of Operation
9:00 a.m. - 5:00 p.m. Tuesday - Sunday, March 1 - November 30; 9:00 a.m. - 5:00 p.m. Saturday and Sunday, December 1 - February 28; closed Thanksgiving, Christmas, and New Year's Day

Admission Fee
$1.75 adults, $1.25 students, military or retired; 25% discount for groups of 10 or more; special fee for groups of 25-1000

Reservations
Requested for special programs and required for groups.

FORT JACKSON — 2

Fort Jackson
1 Fort Jackson Road
Savannah, GA 31404
telephone 912/232-3945

Fort Jackson, Georgia's oldest standing fort, is a 3-mile drive from downtown Savannah. Its location on the Savannah River channel made it important in the military history of the city. Today the Coastal Heritage Society, a non-profit organization, is operating Old Fort Jackson to ensure the preservation of coastal Georgia's historical heritage through programs of active public involvement. A self-guided tour takes approximately ½ to 1 hour.

Originally a brickyard, the site was manned during the American Revolution, but was soon abandoned due to malaria, thereby allowing the British to sail up the river and capture Savannah. In 1808 the United States government purchased the land and designed a heavy artillery position to protect the City of Savannah. During the Civil War, Fort Jackson became the headquarters for the river batteries operated by the Confederates.

Fort Jackson offers a slide show depicting the military history of Savannah and special event programs demonstrating cannon-firing, blacksmithing, and musketry. The museum at Fort Jackson uses cells, guard rooms, offices, and store rooms in the fort to house exhibits on fort construction, uniforms, flags, and military shipping. Also found are cannons, a boat shed with dugout and tools, a blacksmith forge, and the oldest known portable steam engine.

Fort Jackson reenacts the living history of coastal Georgia during its special events. The physical structure of the fort and its historical function will appeal to the history buff, and the staff will go to great lengths to make history come alive for children. On Saturday evenings in June, July and August, a special 2-½ hour program titled "trooping of the colors" presents the military history of the fort.

FORT MCALLISTER — 3

Fort McAllister & Richmond Hill State Park
Georgia Department of Natural Resources
Richmond Hill State Park
Route 2, Box 394-A
Richmond Hill, GA 31324
telephone 912/727-2339

Fort McAllister is perched on the southern bank of the picturesque Ogeechee River. This fort was the southernmost unit of the fortifications that once guarded Savannah from attack mounted from the water. In December of 1864 the fall of Fort McAllister marked the end of Sherman's "March to the Sea."

The earthwork fort proved to be more resilient to bombardment from Union naval forces than were masonry forts like Fort Pulaski. Each night following the barrage of cannon fire, the sand ramparts were repaired by soldiers and slaves. Sherman finally had to resort to taking the fort physically in hand-to-hand combat.

In the 1930's, Henry Ford acquired the property and immediately undertook massive restoration. In 1958, the International Paper Co. bought the site and deeded it to the State of

Special Events
Memorial Day; Labor Day; Scottish Games first Saturday in May; Christmas season program

Directions
Get off I-95 at exit 17. Take I-16 east to Savannah; I-16 ends at Montgomery Street. Proceed to Bay Street and turn right. Proceed on Bay to President Street Extension (U.S. Hwy. 80). The entrance is approximately 2 miles on the left.

Facilities
- *boat facilities*
   docking
   launch
- *brochures*
- *camping*
   primitive, for organizations
   intermediate
   recreational vehicle
- *exhibits*
- *guided tours, by prior arrangement*
- *handicapped access, limited*
- *interpretive programs*
- *museum*
- *pets on leash only*
- *picnic areas*
- *rest areas*
- *restrooms*
- *visitor contact station*

Hours of Operation
Fort McAllister Museum 9:00 a.m. - 5:00 p.m. Tuesday - Saturday, 2:00 p.m. - 5:30 p.m. Sunday; closed Mondays (except federal holidays) Christmas, and Thanksgiving

Richmond Hill State Park 7:00 a.m. - 10:00 a.m. daily year-round.

Admission Fee
Fort McAllister Museum $1.50 adults, $ .75 children over 5 yrs; group rates $1.25 person, $ .50 per student on school bus

Richmond Hill State Park — fee for camping

Reservations
Fort McAllister Museum: interpretive programs and special tours available by prior arrangement

Richmond Hill State Park: camping reservations taken up to 30 days in advance; $5 non-refundable reservation fee

Special Events
Last weekend of July "Baptism by Fire;" Labor Day weekend "Labor Day Encampment;" first weekend of December "Winter Muster"

Directions
Get off I-95 at exit #15, and proceed on GA Hwy. 144 east for approximately 6 miles. Turn left on Spur 144 and continue 4.5 miles to the park and museum.

Fort McAllister — continued

Georgia. The Georgia Historic Commission continued the work of restoration, bringing the sandy earthworks and the "bombproofs" to a state which was close to the condition of 1865.

The result of the efforts of restoration is an area in which ecology and history mingle to the delight of visitors of all ages. Students of the Civil War years in particular will discover much to enhance their learning.

Today, Fort McAllister, with its scenic surroundings of pine woods, tidal river, oyster banks, marshlands, and cabbage palmetto trees, plays host to human guests as well as countless wildlife inhabitants. Summertime visitors will find more rangers on hand for guided tours and more special events planned than will winter tourists, although the fort is open all year. The last weekend of July offers a reenactment called "Baptism by Fire," and on Labor Day visitors can participate in the "Labor Day Encampment."

Wintertime visitors will find a marked decrease in annoying insects, camping at its best, good bird-watching, and on the first weekend of December a two-day event called the "Winter Muster" commemorating the end of Sherman's "March to the Sea."

The atmosphere here is one of friendly interest. Rangers will share with the visitor a detailed knowledge of the area, its ecology and history, and, upon advance notice, will arrange guided tours. The museum offers a good introduction to the fort and provides an abundance of printed material, including an encapsulated history for the tourist on the run, and a self-guided tour sheet for those who may want to explore on their own. The museum is small, but an annex offers a movie introducing the history of the fort.

Ample picnic grounds and play areas provide families with a place for rest and refreshment. Camping facilities also include a dock from which to crab, fish, or shrimp. Crabbing and shrimping are best in late summer.

Fort McAllister Historic Site and Richmond Hill State Park are adjacent to one another, and both are run by the Department of Natural Resources. The Park provides the recreational support (picnic area, camping, boat ramps) for the historic features of Fort McAllister. They do have slightly different hours of operation. Please note this in the legend. Currently, legislation is being considered to combine Fort McAllister and Richmond Hill State Park under one name, Fort McAllister Historic Park.

There are tours available to nearby Richmond Hill and Midway which are of historic interest; pamphlets are available at the museum. Campers and fishermen may replenish supplies at Fort McAllister Supply House, which is just outside the site.

All in all, every element combines at Fort McAllister to insure a stimulating, inspiring, and comfortable experience.

FORT PULASKI NATIONAL MONUMENT — 4

Fort Pulaski National Monument
National Park Service
P. O. Box 98
Tybee Island, GA 31328
telephone 912/786-5787

An easy half-hour drive from Savannah, Fort Pulaski offers the visitor an impressive historic experience as well as a close-up view of life in the salt marsh. Run by the National Park Service, this site provides a pleasant family outing throughout the year. In summer, live Civil War demonstrations occur daily. School-age children will enjoy seeing 19th-century life in a fort, learning of the rigorous life led by its soldiers, and seeing the pock-marked wall where Civil War bombardment occurred. However, the soldiers' life was influenced more by disease, insects, limited food, and boredom than by fighting. The bombardment by federal troops in 1862 with rifled cannons changed fort construction techniques forever. Surrounded by a moat

Facilities
- boat facilities launch
- brochures and lists of bird species
- demonstrations
- exhibits
- handicapped access
- museum
- pets on leash only
- picnic area
- restrooms
- trails, marked
- visitor center

Hours of Operation
8:30 a.m. - 5:30 p.m. daily, after Labor Day until Memorial Day; 8:30 a.m. - 6:45 p.m. daily, from Memorial Day to Labor Day; closed Christmas and New Years Day.

Admission Fee
March 1 - October 31, $1.00 per person or $3.00 per car maximum; persons 16 and under or 62 and older free; tour groups charged per person rate

Special Events
April 10-11 Anniversary of the Siege of Fort Pulaski, August 25 Anniversary of the founding of the National Park Service, October 11 Casimir Pulaski Day, December 26 Confederate Candlelight Open House

Reservations
Special tours and special demonstrations require two weeks advance notice.

Directions
Get off I-95 at exit 17 and take I-16 east to Savannah; I-16 ends at Montgomery Street. Proceed to Bay Street and turn right. Proceed on Bay to the President Street Extension (U.S. Highway 80). Drive east for approximately 18 miles (President Street Extension becomes the Islands Expressway and then Tybee Road). The entrance to the fort is on the left.

which gives a castle-like appearance, the fort has catacombs to explore where food and ammunition were kept.

Named after Revolutionary War hero Count Casimir Pulaski, the fort was begun in 1829 to guard the two entrances to the Savannah River. A young officer named Robert E. Lee found his first military assignment here after graduating from West Point. The construction of a masonry fort on top of highly unstable marsh soil required special skill and this can still be seen today in such features as the uniform line of bricks at the water line of the moat around the fort. Not visible, but interpreted in the visitor center, are the elaborate underpinnings that were necessary to support the fort's enormous weight.

Located on Cockspur Island (so named because of the shape of its dangerous reef that juts out into the open sound) Fort Pulaski offers excellent opportunities to view the coastal salt marsh closely. The fort has three trails for the nature buff — the island trail (1/4 mile), the nature trail (1/2 mile), and the dike system circuit walk. These shallow water environments provide the only source of freshwater for most island wildlife. Periodically, they produce rich blooms of aquatic plants, fish, frogs, and other species, and thus are important in most island food chains.

A small monument to John Wesley, founder of Methodism, is located in a clearing off one of the paths. There are the remains of some old fortifications and gun emplacements along the trails.

A granite pier, once used for unloading supplies, is now surrounded by salt marsh and the special vegetation that thrives in the transition zone between salt marsh and high ground. With the exception of the salt marsh, which makes up more than half the total National Monument area, Cockspur Island is manmade. It exists today as a result of dikes and drainage canals built in association with fort construction and as a result of dredged material being taken from the Savannah River and deposited on the marsh. Cockspur's trees and shrub communities grow on top of these manmade features.

This site has general family appeal and unusual features of the environment. Its picnic area and proximity to Tybee Island allow an expansion of a family outing into a day-long affair. The facilities are attractive and the visitor center is one of the best on the coast.

MARINE EXTENSION CENTER — 5

University of Georgia Marine Extension Service
P. O. Box 13687
Savannah, GA 31416
telephone 912/356-2496

Situated on a bluff overlooking the Skidaway River, the Marine Extension Center is located on Skidaway Island, approximately 15 miles from downtown Savannah. The center shares a 680-acre campus with the Skidaway Institute of Oceanography, which is a marine research arm of the University System of Georgia. The Marine Extension Center offers a variety of marine science educational activities.

The individual visitor and families are welcome year-round to tour the aquarium and exhibits depicting marine life and coastal resources. This aquarium is the most extensive on the Georgia coast. The fish and other marine organisms maintained in the aquarium are those native to Georgia and adjacent coastal waters. One particularly interesting exhibit features Gray's Reef. Also housed within the center is an archaeological exhibit representing a time span of 12,000 years. Mammoths, skulls of extinct whales, and shark teeth are featured among the many fossils.

Visitors are on their own as they tour the Marine Extension Center, but staff members are available to speak to groups if appropriate arrangements are made in advance. The site is now marked with trails, and visitors are welcome to picnic and enjoy the view of the Skidaway

Facilities
- *aquarium, 10,000 gallon marine*
- *environmental education study sites*
- *exhibits*
- *field trips, by prior arrangement*
- *interpretive programs, by prior arrangement*
- *restrooms*

Hours of Operation
9:00 a.m. - 4:00 p.m. Monday - Friday, 12 noon - 5 p.m. Saturday and Sunday; closed Christmas week, New Years Day, Labor Day, July 4th, and Thanksgiving

Admission Fee
For special programs

Reservations
Required for special programs, at least two weeks in advance

Directions

Exit I-95 at exit #16. Drive 12 miles north on GA Hwy. 204. Turn right onto Montgomery Crossroads. Proceed 1.4 miles (three traffic lights) and turn right onto Whitfield Avenue (this becomes Diamond Causeway). Proceed 8 miles from the 4-way stop intersection with Ferguson Avenue, going across the Diamond Causeway to Skidaway Island, and past both entrances to The Landings.

Facilities
- *exhibits*
- *handicapped access, limited*
- *interpretive programs, by prior arrangement*
- *lodging, for groups only*
- *museum*
- *pets on leash only*
- *restrooms*
- *special programs/events, by prior arrangement*
- *tours, guided by prior arrangement*
- *trail, marked*

River. A visit to the center can be completed in an hour's time. Skidaway Island State Park is a short drive away and would provide additional activities for a day's jaunt.

For the educator or group leader, the Marine Extension Service offers a wide range of educational programs including elementary and secondary programs, teacher workshops, and short courses for science and engineering professionals. Visits may range in length from an hour or two (for a guided tour of the aquarium and exhibits) to a full week (for a complete unit on marine science). Programs include dock and marsh studies, historical studies, films and barrier island studies, as well as a trip to Wassaw Island. There is a wide range of facilities available to study groups, or groups who are interested in having a conference oriented to coastal issues. Reservations should be made well in advance. Spring dates are usually booked 4-6 months in advance.

For a short visit or extended group activity, a trip to the Marine Extension Center is definitely worth the time. This center provides a rare opportunity to glimpse underwater life and to begin to grasp the delicate balance in which nature thrives.

NEW EBENEZER — 6
THE GEORGIA SALZBURGER SOCIETY MUSEUM
JERUSALEM LUTHERAN CHURCH

Family Retreat and Recreation Center
Route 1, Box 478
Rincon, GA 31326
telephone 912/754-9242, museum: 912/754-6333

Thirty miles up the Savannah River is what remains of the town of Ebenezer: the Jerusalem Lutheran Church, the old cemetery, the Georgia Salzburger Society Museum, and a new recreation center. The isolated surprise of this site in the midst of the woods is a delightful step back in time.

Founded by Lutherans from Salzburg seeking religious freedom, the town of Ebenezer was established in 1734. Two years later, the community moved to a bluff on the Savannah River and called itself New Ebenezer. In 1769 the beautiful Jerusalem Lutheran Church was built of bricks made from nearby clay deposits and is the oldest public building still standing in Georgia. It was this church which founded the first orphanage in Georgia. Nearby is the cemetery with monuments to the active members of the Ebenezer community.

The museum preserves the culture that once thrived here, displaying furniture, clothing, tools, books, and toys used by the settlers. The hours and days of operation are limited, so plan your trip accordingly. Near the museum is an old cabin similar to ones used by the early settlers, and it is open for tours.

The Family Retreat and Recreation Center is available to church groups, family reunions, scouts, and school groups. The center is built to reflect the environment of the 18th century, and a pleasant nature walk is in the retreat area.

The natural setting of the Ebenezer church and museum is a large part of its charm. Beautiful oaks, dogwood, flame azaleas, and bald cypress trees are captivating, and lend an air of serenity to the visitor. For a few moments of tranquility and a glimpse of the past, a visit to Ebenezer can be quite rewarding.

Hours of Operation
Museum: 3:00 p.m. - 5:00 p.m. Wednesday, Saturday and Sunday; Family Retreat and Recreation Center: year-round; church: 11:00 a.m. Sunday service

Admission Fee
Museum: donations appreciated; Family Retreat and Recreation Center: contact for current information

Reservations
Museum: advisable; Family Retreat and Recreation Center: required (Route 1, Box 478, Rincon, GA 31326; telephone 912/754-9242)

Directions
Exit I-95 at exit #19. Take GA Hwy. 21 north to GA Hwy. 275 between Rincon and Springfield. Turn right on GA Hwy. 275 and proceed approximately 6 miles. New Ebenezer is on the Savannah River at the deadend of GA Hwy. 275.

OATLAND ISLAND EDUCATION CENTER — 7

Facilities
- *brochures and trail guide*
- *demonstrations*
- *exhibits*
- *handicapped access, limited*
- *interpretive programs, by prior arrangement for school groups*
- *restrooms*
- *special events/programs*
- *study sites*
- *trails, marked*
- *visitor contact station*

Hours of Operation
8:30 a.m.-5:00 p.m. Monday-Friday, 11:00 a.m. - 5:00 p.m. second Saturday of each month from October through May; closed Christmas, Easter, and July 4th.

Admission Fee
Can of Alpo dog food, cat food, or bird seed.

Directions
Exit I-95 at exit #17 and proceed to Savannah on I-16. I-16 ends at Montgomery Street. Proceed to Bay Street and turn right. Proceed on Bay Street to the President Street Extension (U.S. Hwy. 80); this becomes the Islands Expressway. Approximately 1 mile after crossing the Wilmington River Bridge, turn right onto Barley Drive and proceed to the main gate of the center.

Oatland Island Education Center
Savannah-Chatham Board of Education
711 Sandtown Road
Savannah, GA 31410
telephone 912/897-3773

Oatland Island Education Center, located just 15 minutes from downtown Savannah, is a most unusual education center, unique not only to Savannah, but to the entire state. The maritime forest camouflages natural habitats for animals native to the Georgia coast, such as deer, timber wolves, panthers, black bears, bobcats, the bald eagle, hawks, owls, and alligators. Woodland trails allow the visitor to observe these animals with minimum disturbance to their daily routine. Oatland also houses The Georgia Conservancy's coastal office, and interested persons are welcome to stop by the office located in the main building.

Upon entering Oatland's gates, the visitor will notice a sign which says, "Slow — Watch for Crossing Animals." This is a clue to Oatland's desire to allow the roaming animals as much freedom as possible and also to permit the interaction of children and other visitors with these animals. Sheep with heavy coats, black-faced Nubian goats, shaggy-maned Shetland ponies, and a pair of white geese may inquisitively inspect the visitor as they roam about the grounds of Oatland. A recalcitrant mule is occasionally pressed into service to help grind sugar cane at the annual craft festival staged each November at the authentic 19th century cabins tucked into the woods.

In September, 1974, Oatland Island Education Center opened under the auspices of the Chatham County Board of Education. The very dedicated staff of environmental educators has forged an important legacy for all Chatham County schoolchildren as well as for residents of coastal Georgia and visitors. The buildings and grounds once functioned as a retirement home for the Brotherhood of Railroad Conductors, then as a public health hospital, and then as the Technical Development Laboratories for the Center for Disease Control.

The center now encompasses 175 acres of pine and maritime forest, open fields, and salt marsh which afford many different opportunities for "hands-on" environmental education. Within this acreage are the habitat compounds for a number of animals, as well as a small farmyard with a cow, pigs, chickens, rabbits, and goats.

Visiting school groups are treated to an interpretive guided tour of the center, but they may also participate in programs such as forest study, marsh transects, solar power, marine and estuarine ecology, freshwater pond study, invertebrate and botanical studies, orienteering (compass), and indoor laboratory studies. In addition to all of these various programs, Oatland has two observatories that house 10- and 16-inch reflector telescopes, and a media center complete with audio-visual equipment and a television studio.

The public is welcome to visit this fascinating and educational area Monday through Friday. Tours on these days are self-guided. Every second Saturday, from October through May, "Saturday at Oatland" features special programs, demonstrations, interpretive programs, and guided nature walks for the general public showing how much fun education can really be.

OSSABAW ISLAND — 8

Ossabaw Island
Island Manager
Georgia Department of Natural Resources
P. O. Box 14565
Savannah, GA 31416
telephone 912/485-2251

Directions
No transportation is provided. A visitor must have a boat; located in Ossabaw Sound between Wassaw Island and St. Catherines Island.

Ossabaw Island is an island of approximately 11,800 acres with 9.5 miles of sandy, beautiful beach. This v-shaped island is not open to the general public. The beach itself is open during the daylight hours only to those who have a boat and want to picnic, but the interior of the island is not open to the general public without permission.

Ossabaw Island's early history mirrors that of many of Georgia's other barrier islands. It was first used as a hunting and fishing area by coastal Indians, then became the site of a Spanish mission, and later became the home of large colonial plantations. What makes Ossabaw remarkable is its more recent past. Beginning in 1961, Ossabaw was the site of several exceptional programs designed to share the island's resources without significantly altering them.

The Ossabaw Island Project invited qualified people in the arts, humanities, sciences, and other professions to work without interruption. A true interdisciplinary program, this project brought together musicians, ecologists, sculptors, authors, and others to pursue their work and exchange ideas.

The Genesis Project, part of the Ossabaw Island Project, was an opportunity for students to work on independent projects while living in a small, interdisciplinary, cooperative community. Students representing over 20 colleges and universities participated in the project which included studies of Ossabaw's plants, animals, and ecosystems. Due to a lack of funds, this program is no longer in operation.

Most importantly, Ossabaw offers a lesson in how preservation of significant natural areas can be accomplished through a cooperative effort between private landowners, state agencies, and private conservation organizations. Motivated by a desire to protect the island from development, Eleanor West, owner of half the island, initiated discussions which resulted in the ultimate purchase of Ossabaw by the State of Georgia in 1978. Ossabaw Island was dedicated as a Heritage Preserve made possible by the Georgia Heritage Trust Act of 1975. This dedication provides for the protection, conservation, and preservation of the natural and cultural resources of the island for the benefit of present and future generations. As a Heritage Preserve, Ossabaw is only to be used for natural, scientific, and cultural purposes based on environmentally sound practices. The proper management of the island is the responsibility of the

Opossum

Georgia Department of Natural Resources. Mrs. West retains a life estate to a portion of Ossabaw Island and occasionally, permission is granted through the Ossabaw Foundation, to selected organizations and groups, to visit the interior of the island. Requests should be sent to: Public Use and Education, The Ossabaw Foundation, Ossabaw Island, P. O. Box 13397, Savannah, GA 31416-0397.

Future use will be managed by the Department of Natural Resources in keeping with the guidelines established by the Heritage Trust Act.

Ossabaw Foundation projects are based on the premise that people must understand their relationship to the environment, and they should "look at everything before disturbing anything." Future state public access plans will hopefully be true to this premise and should be based on a thorough study and understanding of the fragile and vulnerable nature of the island's environments prior to public use decisions.

SAVANNAH NATIONAL WILDLIFE REFUGE — 9

Savannah National Wildlife Refuge
U.S. Fish & Wildlife Service
Savannah Coastal Refuges
P. O. Box 8487
Savannah, GA 31412
telephone 912/944-4415

The family seeking a few hours of peaceful relaxation in beautiful out-of-doors surroundings, or the dedicated naturalist, birder, botanist, or canoeist will find this spot as much a refuge for humans as it is for the bald eagle and other protected birds and beasts. The contrast between city and country is heightened by glimpses of the Savannah industrial and port complexes silhouetted across marshlands and river.

Facilities
- *brochures*
- *exhibit shelter*
- *handicapped access, limited*
- *pets on leash only*
- *restrooms*
- *special events/programs*
- *trails, marked and unmarked*
      bicycle
      driving
      walking

Hours of Operation
Hours vary monthly but generally open 30 minutes after sunrise until 30 minutes before sunset.

Directions

Exit I-95 at U.S. Hwy. 17, exit #5, in Hardeeville, SC. Follow U.S. Hwy. 17 towards Savannah. Bear right at fork and continue on U.S. Hwy. 17 toward the Airport. The refuge entrance (Laurel Hill Wildlife Drive) is approximately 2 miles on the left.

From Savannah take U.S. Hwy. 17A across the Talmadge Bridge. Drive approximately 8 miles to the intersection of U.S. Hwy. 17 and 17A. Turn left and follow U.S. Hwy. 17 south towards the Airport. The refuge entrance (Laurel Hill Wildlife Drive) is approximately 2 miles on the left.

The introduction to the wildlife refuge is just inside the entrance where an exhibit shelter has been built. This shelter contains leaflet dispensers, maps and booklets. The visitor should be sure to walk around to the back of the shelter, where there are additional leaflets and printed material. The area surrounding the shelter is a pleasant site for a picnic, although there are no tables or facilities provided.

The Laurel Hill Wildlife Drive begins just inside the entrance and continues for five miles. It is open to the hiker, the bicyclist, and to private cars, which allow visitors in wheelchairs to view the wildlife without venturing into the refuge's more remote areas. The official speed limit for motorists is 20 mph, but there is so much to see that a driver may not always attain that speed. Visitors must be alert on the wildlife drive, for it is possible to gaze across a stream for fifteen minutes and fail to spot a young alligator sunning itself on a mudbank. With patience, skill and luck, the most amateur of watchers may catch sight of a bald eagle, an otter, deer, or other shy creatures.

A fascinating mini-hike off the drive is the Cistern Trail which loops through Recess Island. The trail is clearly marked. A convenient parking lot allows motorists to enjoy this waterside promenade.

There are thirty-nine miles of dikes open to hikers and bird watchers. For the canoeist, there are bottomland hardwoods accessible by tidal creeks branching from the Savannah River. Boat access into this swampland can be gained from several state-maintained landings on the Savannah River. For historians, there is the history of the old Savannah plantations and their rice culture lore. Photographers are furnished with waterfowl in winter and gallinules, wood ducks, and wading birds in summer. Naturalists will find plants, animals, birds, butterflies, trees, reptiles, amphibians and wildflowers to study and appreciate.

The sportsman can fish and hunt waterfowl, feral hogs, deer, and squirrel during special seasons. The dates for these hunts may vary each year. The Savannah Coastal Refuges office should be contacted for dates and to receive the required permit to take part in the managed hunts. Only hunters with the appropriate permits will be allowed on the refuge. Hunters must obtain all licenses required by the state in which they hunt (Georgia and/or South Carolina). For safety reasons the refuge is closed to the general public when hunts are scheduled. Although hunts take place only six or seven days out of the year, when planning a fall or winter visit, call ahead to determine whether or not a hunt is occurring.

The dikes that connect with the tour route are open to hikers. The Tupelo-Swamp Walk which extends east of the northernmost pool (Pool #1), bordered by the Vernezobre Creek, provides the best retreat for bird watchers and photographers. This walk can be reached by walking 2 miles north from U.S. Hwy. 17 along the east dike paralleling the freshwater diversion canal. (The location of the Tupelo-Swamp Walk is marked on the map posted in the exhibit shelter at the wildlife drive entrance.) Access, however, may sometimes be closed to prevent disturbance to waterfowl.

This refuge provides a quick escape from Savannah or Hilton Head Island, and the visitor will find a variety of wildlife, including a possible bobcat, or hear the bone-rattling bellow of an alligator in the spring. This is also one of the few places where one can observe dikes and "trunks" (water control structures) that were used for rice cultivation in the 19th century.

SAVANNAH SCIENCE MUSEUM — 10

Savannah Science Museum
4405 Paulsen Street
Savannah, GA 31405
telephone 912/355-6705

The Savannah Science Museum provides a wealth of learning experiences for the one-time visitor or the resident of Savannah. Geared for all ages, the museum has a planetarium with a

Facilities
- *brochures*
- *demonstrations, by prior arrangement*
- *exhibits*
- *handicapped access*
- *interpretive program, by prior arrangement*
- *restrooms*
- *special events/programs*
- *soft drink machine*
- *tours, by prior arrangement*

Hours of Operation
10:00 a.m. - 5:00 p.m., Tuesday - Saturday, year-round, 2:00 p.m. - 5:00 p.m. Sunday; closed Mondays, July 4th, Thanksgiving, Christmas, and New Years Day
Note: Planned renovations may change these hours; call ahead

Admission Fee
$1.00 adults, $ .50 children and senior citizens, free for members

Reservations
Required for groups

Directions
Exit I-95 at #17. Proceed on I-16 toward Savannah. Exit I-16 at Lynes Parkway south (I-516). Lynes Parkway becomes DeRenne Avenue at the first traffic light. Proceed east on DeRenne to the sixth traffic light. Turn left onto Paulsen Street, and proceed approximately one mile to the museum on the left.

full-time planetarium director. The planetarium has regular programs which are open to the public every Sunday at 3:00 p.m. The museum also houses one of the Southeast's largest reptile and amphibian collections consisting of representative samples of the 189 species of snakes, lizards, turtles, alligators, salamanders, frogs, and toads which are found in Georgia. The museum features exhibits of live poisonous and non-poisonous snakes found in Georgia, reference collections of Indian-Pacific Ocean shells, rocks and minerals indigenous to Georgia, and a pressed herbarium collection of over 2000 species of Georgia plants.

The Science Museum was founded by the American Association of University Women who felt that Savannah needed a natural history museum to supplement educational programs. The museum opened its doors in 1958, and today is self-supported by educational programs, memberships, and grants. On the second Sunday of each month the museum is open free of charge to visitors courtesy of the City of Savannah.

The building which houses the museum is in itself unique for it has the second largest solar unit in the state, providing air conditioning, heat, and hot water. The solar powered unit is designed for display as well as practical use.

The Science Museum, in cooperation with the U.S. Fish & Wildlife Service, also sponsors the Caretta Research Project, a hands-on volunteer-oriented project aimed at protecting the threatened loggerhead sea turtle. Volunteers patrol the beaches of Wassaw Island in the summer months, searching for nesting female loggerheads to tag. Eggs laid by the massive sea turtles are then transported to a hatchery for protection from predators and beach erosion. Those interested in participating should contact the director of the Caretta Research Project at the museum.

In addition to its many exhibits, the Science Museum also offers, by special arrangement to groups and individuals, the opportunity to visit its property on the Ogeechee River. This tract is in an undisturbed sandhill and river ecosystem and is described in more detail in the following narrative.

The Savannah Science Museum also has the added bonus of a gift shop oriented toward science with low-priced items that make good stocking stuffers or souvenirs.

SAVANNAH SCIENCE MUSEUM'S OGEECHEE RIVER PROPERTY — 11

Savannah Science Museum
4405 Paulsen Street
Savannah, GA 31405
telephone 912/355-6705

Facilities
• *trails*

Hours of Operation
Daylight hours, year-round

Reservations
Advanced permission must be obtained from the Savannah Science Museum

Directions
Obtain from the Savannah Science Museum

This property, owned by the Savannah Science Museum, is one of the best places to observe a unique combination of environmental communities — the river dune ridge community and the lowland hardwood swamp. The Ogeechee River runs along the southern boundary of this 170-acre tract. The property is separated from the river by a hardwood swamp of bald cypress and tupelo trees, so it is difficult to see the main channel of the river from here.

The river dune ridge community supports a dwarf oak-evergreen shrub forest with a lichen floor. One of the most interesting plants in this ecosystem is the drawf live oak, stunted by the nutrient-poor soil.

There are three obvious old roads that run through the property as well as numerous unmarked trails. The approach trail, however, is subject to flooding in early spring. Mid-spring, when the wild azaleas are blooming, is a wonderful time to visit. Numerous wildflowers can be seen in summer and in winter. The sandhill community can be enjoyable as well as educational.

This site is actually best suited to school groups, botanists, naturalists, or photographers, and not to the average tourist. The property is very accessible except during spring floods and is in an area where almost all the sandhills have been developed or cleared and planted in pine. Permission to visit the property can and must be obtained by calling the Savannah Science Museum.

Facilities
- brochures and lists of bird and plant species
- camping
    primitive
    intermediate
    recreational vehicle
- demonstrations
- exhibits
- food and beverage
    concession in summer
    vending machines
- guided tours (by prior arrangement)
- handicapped access
- interpretive programs
- pets on leash only
- picnic areas
- restrooms
- rest areas
- special events/programs
- study sites
- swimming pool
- trails, marked
- visitor center

Hours of Operation
7:00 a.m. - 10:00 p.m. 7 days a week, year-round

SKIDAWAY ISLAND STATE PARK — 12

Skidaway Island State Park
Georgia Department of Natural Resources
Savannah, GA 31406
telephone 912/356-2523

Skidaway Island State Park, rich in cultural, archaeological, and ecological treasures, is one of the best camping spots in the Savannah area. A day's outing for nearby residents promises hiking, fishing, boating, or picnics. The park is located on a twelve-mile square Pleistocene island, which is separated from the Atlantic Ocean by a vast expanse of marsh and Wassaw Island. Skidaway Island State Park borders Skidaway Narrows. Skidaway Narrows was at one time a small, shallow creek in the salt marsh that was first dredged by the Army Corps of Engineers in 1905 and later dredged to become part of today's Atlantic Intracoastal Waterway.

Within the park are the vegetation and wildlife of a maritime forest. Tidal creeks, salt marsh, and forest abound with sights and sounds of interest to the bird watcher, naturalist, and camera enthusiast. There are freshwater wetlands in the park which are important to wildlife, such as deer and raccoon. Painted buntings (in breeding season), pileated woodpeckers, and a variety of shore and wading birds may be seen by the observant and quiet hiker.

A twenty minute walk along the Sandpiper Trail takes the visitor by fiddler crabs in the salt marshes, island hammocks, and yaupon holly and cabbage palmetto trees. In the early spring, the Cherokee rose, the state flower of Georgia, is in bloom. The Sandpiper Trail also affords a view of unique salt flats. During the Civil War, the coastal islands and the marshes formed natural barriers against enemy raids. Also on the Sandpiper Trail are the remains of Confederate earthworks used to defend Savannah.

During the summer months there is a regular schedule of interpretive programs at the park. Programs during other seasons may be arranged by writing or telephoning park personnel. There is also a swimming pool at the park with a lifeguard on duty. Only five minutes from the park is a boat launch into the Intracoastal Waterway.

Other sites near the park include Wormsloe Historic Site and the Marine Extension Center. Historic Savannah is only thirty minutes from the park, so the visitor will find a short stay or an extended visit full of promise.

Reservations
Some available for camping and group shelters; contact park office 8:00 a.m. - 5:00 p.m.

Admission Fee
Fee for camping, shelters and pool

Directions
Exit from I-95 at exit #16. Proceed toward Savannah 12 miles. Turn right onto Montgomery Crossroads and proceed 1.4 miles to Whitfield Avenue (third traffic light). Turn right onto Whitfield Avenue (becomes Diamond Causeway) and proceed 5 miles to the entrance of the park.

TUCKASSEE KING LANDING — 13

This public boat ramp on a creek 200 yards from the Savannah River is located beside a picturesque mesic bluff 75 to 100 feet high. A mesic bluff is a tablelike, flat-topped bluff formed by river erosion many years ago. For the boater, botanist, or nature buff, it is a wonderful spot to observe a mesic bluff forest or a bald cypress-tupelo swamp. During the drier months, a hike along the forest floor is inviting.

The Tuckassee King bluff is readily accessible by a paved road and is impressive in its natural beauty and pristine state. This type of bluff is generally uncommon in coastal Georgia due to timber operations and construction of summer cottages. A variety of plants usually found in more northern climates may be observed here, such as liverworts, mosses, and wild ginger. A mesic bluff forest occurs where there is a northern exposure and high moisture content in the soil. Signs of beaver, raccoon, and deer are apparent to the careful observer.

Facilities
- boat facilities
  launch
- pets on leash only

Hours of Operation
Open year-round

Directions
Exit I-95 at exit #19. Proceed north on GA Hwy. 21. Turn right onto GA Hwy. 119 and proceed toward Clyo; 2¾ miles past Clyo turn left from GA Hwy. 119 at the Georgia Historical Marker "Early Baptist at Tuckassee King," and follow road to the boat ramp.

It was here that the early Baptists in coastal Georgia were organized, and a short distance away is an exact replica of the first Baptist church in Georgia.

Unfortunately, Tuckassee King Landing could use some helping hands in cleaning up the site. Providing trash cans for visitors would be helpful. However, only a short distance from Savannah, this is a nice day's trip for a boat outing. It is also a good spot for canoeists searching for a put-in point or take-out point when planning a trip on the Savannah River.

TYBEE ISLAND — 14

Tybee Island
Chamber of Commerce
209 Butler Avenue
Tybee Island, GA 31328
telephone 912/786-5444
museum: 912/786-4077, lighthouse: 912/786-5801

Tybee Island, located just 18 miles east of Savannah, offers the only easily accessible beach on Georgia's northern coast. One can drive to within a few yards of the beach, and parking lots are available at the northern and southern ends of the island. Tybee is also Georgia's most developed barrier island. The city of Tybee consists of a growing number of year-round residences, summer cottages and condominiums, and tourist facilities.

Tybee Island is the best place on the coast to view and study what happens to an island when it has been extensively altered by human activities. By building too close to the ocean, the sand dunes have been destroyed. By building seawalls to protect the property behind them, the beach has suffered. By maintaining a harbor channel to the north, one of the island's sources of sand has been blocked. These, combined with a sea level rise of about 13 inches per century, have contributed to natural erosion processes of substantial magnitude. Over the

Facilities
- bicycle rental
- boat facilities
  charter
  docking
  hoist
  launch
  marina
- brochures
- camping
  intermediate
  recreational vehicle
- exhibits
- food and beverage
- fuel, ice, bait
- handicapped access
- lighthouse
- lodging
  motel/hotel
  rental property
- museum
- pets on leash only; not permitted on beaches
- picnic area
- restrooms
- rest areas
- special events/programs

years, numerous efforts have been made to stem this erosion with jetties, groins, and beach renourishment projects.

One can also learn a great deal about the dynamics of the shore-front at Tybee. In spite of the numerous jetties (some 100 have been built during the last century), seawalls and the restored beach, there are several processes in evidence here, including erosion, accretion, and dune formation. Examples of a relatively natural dune area can be found on 8th and 9th streets, as compared to a seawall supported area found on 2nd Street and 16th Street.

Another area which provides a good view of dune formation processes at work is located at the north end of Tybee. Spanish bayonette and sea oats are quite interesting to see, but do not pick them as they are a protected species of vegetation. From the north end, the stone jetties, Daufuskie and Hilton Head islands are clearly visible. On the same flats pelicans, gulls, and other shorebirds can be seen. But even if one is not interested in the dynamics of beach and dune formation, a trip to Tybee can provide a variety of rewarding experiences.

Originally founded in 1733 by General James Oglethorpe, the Township of Tybee began its role in history with the construction of a lighthouse (the third in America) to guide British ships into Savannah. However, it also served to guide the pirates who plundered the south seas and frequently took refuge in the Savannah River. Blackbeard, one of the more infamous pirates, headquartered his crew in the Tybee area, and it is believed by many that his treasures are still buried beneath the sands of Tybee. In 1779, the French Fleet, the greatest gathering of foreign ships ever assembled in American waters, anchored off Tybee to support the patriots during the siege of Savannah.

Fort Screven, named after a revolutionary war hero, General James Screven, was acquired by the federal government in 1808. Located on the north end of Tybee, the post was enlarged in 1898 and was in continuous use through the end of World War II. In 1945, it was declared surplus and was acquired by the City of Tybee. Now numerous houses are built at the fort including an area called Officer's Row.

Hours of Operation
Beach open year-round; museum: 10:00 a.m. - 6:00 p.m. Monday - Friday, 10:00 a.m. - 5:00 p.m. Saturday and Sunday; lighthouse: 1:00 p.m. - 5:00 p.m. 7 days a week, June 1 - August 31; 1:00 p.m. - 5:00 p.m. Thursday - Monday, September 1 - May 31.

Reservations
Recommended for lodging and camping during peak months

Admission Fee
Museum: $1.00 adults, children 12 and under free, school and scout groups $ .25 per person; lighthouse: $1.00 adults, $ .50 children 6-12 years, school and scout groups $ .25 per person

Directions
Exit I-95 at exit #17 and take I-16 east to Savannah; I-16 ends at Montgomery Street. Proceed to Bay Street and turn right. Proceed on Bay to the President Street Extension (U.S. Hwy. 80). Drive east for approximately 18 miles (President Street Extension becomes the Islands Expressway and Tybee Road).

Both the Tybee Museum and the Tybee Lighthouse are located within the confines of Fort Screven. Visitors may climb to the top of the lighthouse for a wonderful view of the ocean and the island. A tour of the museum can be quite interesting. It offers an eclectic collection of memorabilia ranging from shell collections to Japanese swords to Harper's newspaper reports of various Civil War events. The museum is small and not really geared towards young children. The numerous staircases make passage difficult with strollers and impassable for wheelchairs.

Although these areas are interesting to see, the main attraction of Tybee is definitely the beach and related activities. If one is planning to stay in one of the motels, advance reservations are necessary, especially in the peak summer months. But if planning a day trip with easy accessibility to the beach as well as to refreshments and beach supplies, it is best to visit the south end of Tybee. The north end of Tybee is less accessible (fewer parking spaces and a greater distance to walk to the beach), but it is more scenic and much less crowded.

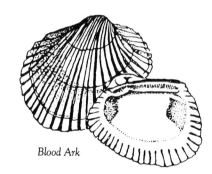
Blood Ark

Camping facilities are also available year-round at the River's End Campground. Reservations are recommended for the fall and necessary for spring and summer. From the tent camper to the largest of recreational vehicles, the River's End has everything for a comfortable experience. Children and families will enjoy the large playground and picnic/cookout area that is located in Memorial Park on Butler Avenue.

For the visitor with his own boat, there is a full line of accommodations. A service marina, open year-round, and boat ramps are located at the south end of the back river. Charter boats for fishing are also available.

For years a popular summer retreat for Savannahians, Tybee Island is one of the few beaches with easy accessibility on the coast of Georgia complete with the usual offerings of a resort. In addition, visitors may catch a view of large foreign freighters entering and leaving the Savannah port.

TYBEE NATIONAL WILDLIFE REFUGE — 15

Tybee National Wildlife Refuge
U.S. Fish & Wildlife Service
Savannah Coastal Refuges
P. O. Box 8487
Savannah, GA 31412
telephone 912/944-4415

Hours of Operation
Public is permitted on the refuge from sunrise to ½ hour after sunset. While nesting is in progress, portions of the refuge may be closed to the public.

Although listed in Savannah Coastal Refuges' brochures, Tybee National Wildlife Refuge is better for birds than bird watchers. This refuge is a sandbar located at the mouth of the Savannah River. The sandbar functions primarily as a spoil disposal site for dredging operations of the U.S. Army Corps of Engineers.

Most of the high ground within the refuge is densely covered with low, scrubby vegetation that is difficult to penetrate. The dense understory encourages a prolific population of rattlesnakes and native rats. The 100-acre site serves as a resting spot for pelicans, seagulls, egrets, and herons. Nesting terns claim a part of the refuge to raise their young.

The U.S. Fish & Wildlife Service does not provide transportation to this island and would-be visitors must rely on their own resources to reach the sandbar. Currents are swift and this site is best viewed from the comfort and safety of one's own boat.

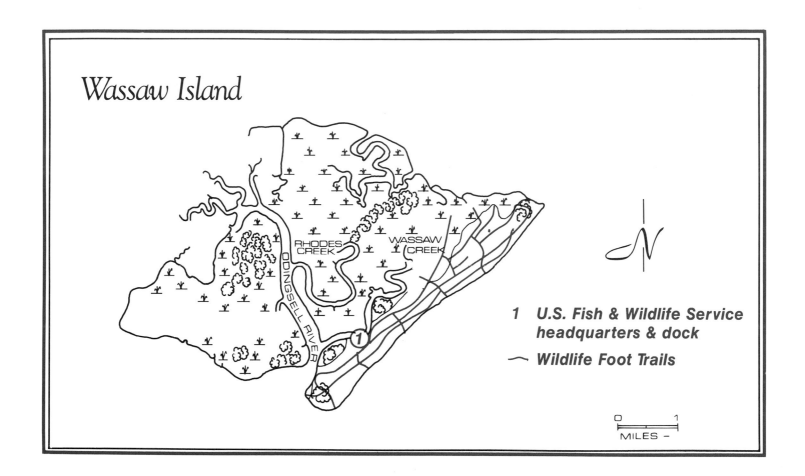

Wassaw Island

RHODES CREEK

WASSAW CREEK

ODINGSELL RIVER

N

1   **U.S. Fish & Wildlife Service headquarters & dock**

⌒   **Wildlife Foot Trails**

0   1
MILES −

WASSAW NATIONAL WILDLIFE REFUGE — 16

Wassaw National Wildlife Refuge
U.S. Fish & Wildlife Service
Savannah Coastal Refuges
P. O. Box 8487
Savannah, GA 31412
telephone 912/944-4415

Wassaw Island, a jewel in Georgia's crown of Golden Isles, is also considered to be the most undeveloped. Very few management practices have altered its natural state through the years, and it is probably one of the best examples of conditions which prevailed before Europeans arrived on the Georgia coast. Accessibility to Wassaw is limited to private and charter boats, although the island is open to the public during daylight hours. (To acquire information on charter services, contact the Savannah Coastal Refuges' office.)

In 1866, Wassaw was purchased by George Parsons, whose family were the first people to spend large amounts of time on the island since the first Indian inhabitants. In 1969, Wassaw was added to the National Wildlife Refuge System as a donation from The Nature Conservancy, which acquired it from the Wassaw Island Trust (established by the descendants of George Parsons). This insured the island's preservation in the face of growing development pressure. The Trust retains a small area in the center of the island and the visitor should respect their privacy.

A special activity on Wassaw is the loggerhead sea turtle project called the Caretta Research Project, which was initiated in 1973. Its purpose on Wassaw is to learn more about the population levels and habits of loggerhead sea turtles and to improve survival rates of loggerhead eggs and hatchlings. Participants in the project observe and tag nesting female turtles and then relocate threatened nests to protected hatchery sites. The nesting and hatching season runs from mid-May through mid-September.

Applications to participate in the Caretta Research Project are accepted through the Savannah Science Museum. (Contact Caretta Research Project Director, 4405 Paulsen Street,

Facilities
- brochures and list of bird species
- exhibit shelter
- trails

Hours of Operation
Daylight hours, only, year-round, except during managed hunts. Portions of Wassaw's beaches may be closed seasonally to prevent disturbance to nesting, wintering, or migrating birds.

Directions
Located 15 miles southeast of Savannah, east of Skidaway Island and south of the Petit Chou Island group.

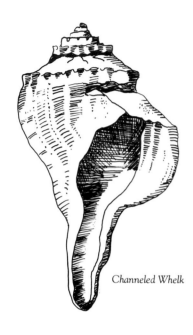

Channeled Whelk

Savannah, Georgia 31405; telephone 912/355-6705.) The Savannah Science Museum works in cooperation with the U.S. Fish and Wildlife Service and the Wassaw Island Trust. This project is the only one in Georgia that relies on volunteers to perpetuate the research, and provides the public with a rare hands-on opportunity to work with a threatened species (those sliding toward man-caused extinction).

Wassaw continues to be the least spoiled of Georgia's barrier islands and provides the public with a variety of wildlife experiences. Special rewards are walking a seven mile stretch of beach — often without encountering another person — that abounds with wildlife. Throughout the year gulls, terns, and a variety of other shorebirds can be seen. During almost all months of the year, a variety of shells and other marine life can be found.

The "boneyard" area of Wassaw's beach is particularly fascinating. Here on the northeast end of the island, erosion has toppled hundreds of live oaks, pines, and cabbage palmettos whose "skeletons" remain strewn along a one mile stretch of beach. This area offers opportunities for photographing these intriguing natural sculptures. Also on the north beach are the remnants of a fort built in 1898 in preparation for the Spanish-American War. The cement, granite, and oyster shell structure consisted of two gun emplacements with an ordinance magazine in between. The fort, once hundreds of feet back from the high tide line, has succumbed to erosion and is partially covered by each tide.

In addition to the usual beach activities, there are over 20 miles of interior island trails through pristine maritime forest that can provide the visitor with an undisturbed wilderness experience. An added bonus is that there are no permits, fees, or guides needed to enjoy the trails; however, federal wildlife refuge regulations must be heeded. Herons, egrets, and other wading birds frequent the ponds and marshes. In the late spring and early summer nesting season, the ponds are rather noisy with the sounds of these birds. During the spring and fall migrations, the woodlands resound with swarms of songbirds passing through coastal Georgia to reach either breeding or wintering grounds. Also during these times the beach hosts huge congregations of migratory shorebirds. Some unusual sightings have also been reported, including a parasitic jaeger and a roseate spoonbill.

There are approximately 180 acres in the middle section of the island that are closed to public use. Owned by the Wassaw Island Trust, this property includes the beach road. The road may be used by the public, but visitors are asked to observe and respect all signs marking closed areas.

Wassaw Island is a fascinating place for visitors who desire all sorts of outdoor experiences from fishing and exploring the beach to the study of barrier island flora and fauna. Boating through the tidal creeks within the refuge's 10,050 acres is a marvelous experience. The marshland can engulf the visitor and create a feeling of total detachment from the noise and confusion of civilization which is, unbelievably, only a 20-minute boat ride away.

WILLIAMSON ISLAND — 17

Office of the Commissioner
Georgia Department of Natural Resources
205 Butler Street, SE
Atlanta, GA 30334
telephone 912/264-7218 (Coastal Resources Division, Brunswick)

Directions
Located south of Tybee Island, north of Wassaw, and east of Little Cabbage Island.

Williamson Island could easily be the most intriguing of all the barrier islands on Georgia's coast, at least for the naturalist. In aerial photos taken in 1957, Williamson Island did not even exist. By 1976, Williamson was an island approximately 250 acres in size with sand dunes covered by sea oats and other grassy vegetation. By 1984 erosional forces had removed more than half of the island, new inlet channels had formed, and it appeared as though the island was moving westward and might fuse into adjacent Petit Chou Island (privately owned). Although access to Williamson Island is tricky, the island offers the unusual experience of observing a young and possibly ephemeral barrier island.

Interestingly enough, Williamson did not emerge from the ocean like the legendary Atlantis, but started as a sand spit off Little Tybee Island. It is believed that this island was probably formed from sand that was once part of Tybee Island.

Williamson Island was first detected as an island in aerial photographs taken in 1971. It continued to grow in subsequent years and was eventually claimed by the State of Georgia as a "new" island. The state submitted this new island to a federal board for naming, which in turn referred it back to the State Board of Natural Resources. Mr. Jimmy Williamson, a former mayor of Darien and a member of the board, had recently passed away, so the island was named in his honor.

As the newest barrier island on the Georgia coast, Williamson is a fascinating study in the ever-changing sand and sea. Its long stretch of white, sandy beach plays host to ghost crabs, hermit crabs, and a variety of shorebirds. Williamson, with an abundance of seashells, offers a chance to observe new sand dunes and their vegetation.

Because only 25 years ago Willamson Island was nothing more than a sandbar, the navigator should approach the island cautiously. Sandbars are constantly shifting, and the waters around Williamson are very shallow. Consult a navigation chart for further information, and observe the tides and currents carefully. Boats behind Williamson have become stranded at low tide and their occupants have been forced to spend an unplanned night waiting for the high tide to arrive.

Although Williamson Island poses an ideal setting in which to study the evolution of an island, at this writing no one is studying the island to determine the natural succession of vegetation. Its stability is also not known. Years from now it may be reclaimed by the ocean as quickly as it was generated.

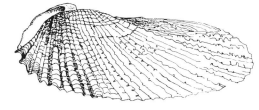

Angel Wing

WORMSLOE HISTORIC SITE — 18

Wormsloe Historic Site
Georgia Department of Natural Resources
7601 Skidaway Road
Savannah, GA 31406
telephone 912/352-2548

Wormsloe Historic Site, an interpretive center on the founding of Georgia, is a 20-minute drive from downtown Savannah. Maintained by the Georgia Department of Natural Resources, Wormsloe provides an enjoyable morning or afternoon outing.

The visitor center contains an excellent 16 minute slide presentation and pictorial history on the colonization of Savannah and featuring the Noble Jones family, owners of Wormsloe Plantation for over two centuries.

The tabby ruins at the site are a pleasant short walk from the center. The ruins are an interesting example of tabby construction and depict a fortified house. Wormsloe was in a strategic position in the defense of Georgia, guarding the former colonial inland waterway passage to Savannah from the south. A gravesite overlooking the salt marsh marks the old burial place of the Noble Jones family.

A mile-long nature trail wanders through woods and over small bridges which span tidal creeks. The trail is carpeted with pine needles and punctuated with posts bearing reproductions of the paintings of Mark Catesby, an early 1700's artist and naturalist. This trail eventually makes a loop around the ruins of the house and gravesite and returns to the museum. Prearranged tours provide special programs conducted by the Living History Interpreters.

Deer, opposums, raccoons, and numerous birds live on Wormsloe, although they may not be visible to large groups of people. Georgia pine, Southern magnolia, dogwood, Spanish bayonet, azalea, and a variety of ferns are abundant, although the character of the forest has been changed by a 1973 outbreak of the Southern pine beetle. In a successful battle to control the

Facilities
- *brochures*
- *demonstrations*
- *exhibits*
- *handicapped access*
- *interpretive programs*
- *museum*
- *pets on leash only*
- *picnic area*
- *restrooms*
- *soft drink machine*
- *special events/programs*
- *study site*
- *tours*
- *trails, marked*
- *visitor contact station*

Hours of Operation
9:00 a.m. - 5:00 p.m. Tuesday - Saturday, 2:00 p.m. - 5:30 p.m. Sunday; closed Mondays (excluding legal holidays), Thanksgiving, and Christmas Day

Admission Fee
$1.50 adults, $ .75 children ages 6-12 yrs.; organized groups of 15 or more, $1.25 adults, $ .50 children.

Reservations
Required in advance for groups and special demonstrations

Directions
Exit I-95 at exit #16. Proceed 12 miles toward Savannah on GA Hwy. 204. Turn right onto Montgomery Crossroads and drive 3.2 miles until the road deadends. Turn right onto Skidaway Road and proceed 0.8 miles to the entrance of the site.

pine beetles' spread, the Georgia Forestry Commission removed the infested trees. As a result, more sunlight reached the forest floor, prompting dense understory growth. This dense foliage would normally occur in a mature forest, but not to the extent that it has at Wormsloe.

The entrance to Wormsloe, with its stone archway and dramatic mile and a half drive of live oaks, makes an impressive and picturesque sight. The Wormsloe home and gardens are privately owned and not open to the public. This historic site is a most accessible and inviting opportunity for a walk through the woods as well as a step back in time.

Mistletoe

CENTRAL COAST

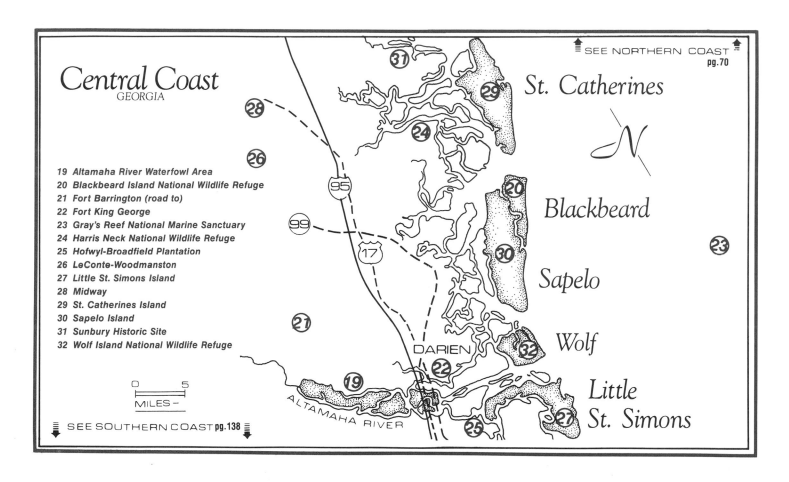

Central Coast
GEORGIA

St. Catherines

N

Blackbeard

Sapelo

Wolf

Little
St. Simons

19 Altamaha River Waterfowl Area
20 Blackbeard Island National Wildlife Refuge
21 Fort Barrington (road to)
22 Fort King George
23 Gray's Reef National Marine Sanctuary
24 Harris Neck National Wildlife Refuge
25 Hofwyl-Broadfield Plantation
26 LeConte-Woodmanston
27 Little St. Simons Island
28 Midway
29 St. Catherines Island
30 Sapelo Island
31 Sunbury Historic Site
32 Wolf Island National Wildlife Refuge

0 5
MILES

SEE SOUTHERN COAST pg.138

DARIEN

ALTAMAHA RIVER

ALTAMAHA RIVER WATERFOWL AREA — 19
Including BUTLER ISLAND and LEWIS ISLAND

Altamaha River Waterfowl Area
Georgia Department of Natural Resources
P. O. Box 19
Sapelo Island, GA 31327
telephone 912/485-2251

Much of the Altamaha River Waterfowl Area is a manipulated habitat designed to provide recreation for the serious fisherman, hunter, bird watcher, and naturalist. The waterfowl area contains 22,000 acres along the Altamaha River near Darien, and boasts the second largest waterfowl area east of the Mississippi, the first being the Chesapeake. Alligators, bobcats, raccoons, herons, egrets, ducks, other wading birds and waterfowl, and an occasional manatee find refuge in the waterfowl area.

The peak season for the bird watcher and the hunter is mid-October through mid-April when the area is flooded to attract waterfowl and wildlife. The bird watcher can hope to see an assortment of ducks such as mallards, black ducks, pintails, gadwalls, wigeons, mergansers, shovelers, green-winged teals, buffleheads, scaup, ring-necks, canvasbacks, as well as some geese. This is one of the few areas on the Atlantic coast where the fulvous tree duck may be seen. The freshwater wetland is filled with giant Southern wildrice, pickerel weed, wild rice, and arrow-arum. The white spider lily is conspicuous when in bloom in late spring and early summer. In the spring and summer, the dikes are allowed to overgrow so that the grasses will seed and provide food for the birds. The visitor should be aware that the waterfowl area is primarily maintained for sport, including that of the hunter; therefore, one should be most cautious during the hunting season.

The waterfowl area includes several islands that are unique and rich in history. Lewis Island boasts magnificent 1,000-year-old bald cypress trees that were saved from the logger's saw due to their remote location in the swamp. The logger would haul trees out of the swamp with cables, but this stand of virgin bald cypress on Lewis Island was out of the cable's reach.

Facilities
- camping
    - primitive
- game checking station

Hours of Operation
8:00 a.m.-4:30 p.m. Monday-Friday; 7 days for hunting September - March; special group arrangements only on holidays

Reservations
Advisable for programs, one week in advance

Directions
Exit I-95 at exit #10. Proceed east on GA Hwy. 251 approximately one mile. Turn right onto U.S. Hwy. 17 south and proceed approximately 2-3 miles through Darien and over the Darien and Butler rivers. Turn right at the checking station approximately 300-400 yards from the bridge.

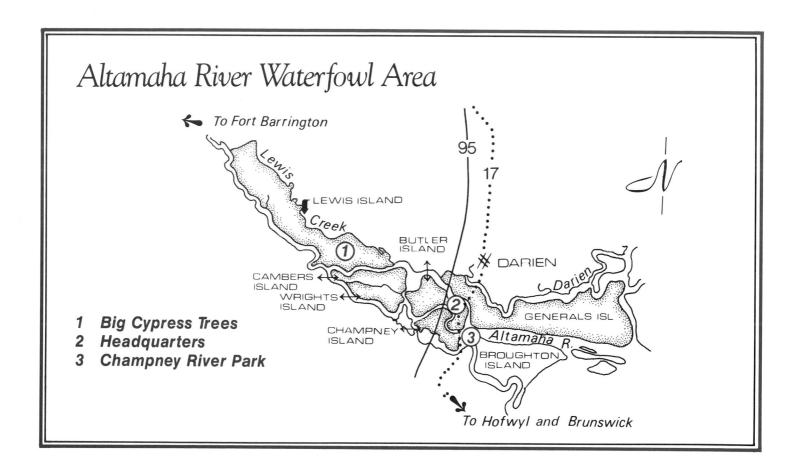

Altamaha River Waterfowl Area

To Fort Barrington

Lewis

LEWIS ISLAND

Creek

BUTLER ISLAND

95

17

DARIEN

Darien

CAMBERS ISLAND

WRIGHTS ISLAND

GENERALS ISL

CHAMPNEY ISLAND

Altamaha R.

BROUGHTON ISLAND

N

1 **Big Cypress Trees**
2 **Headquarters**
3 **Champney River Park**

To Hofwyl and Brunswick

Today the location of these bald cypress trees and river conditions make access difficult. During periods of high water, usually January to June, the Altamaha floods its banks, and Lewis Island is under water. When the river is down, Lewis Island may be approached only by boat. The trail head is located about 1/4 mile southeast of the intersection of Studhorse Creek and Pico Creek. The Department of Natural Resources attempts to keep the trail to the trees well marked, but river floods may have obscured the marks or carried them away. The visitor should ask for directions, landmarks, and river level conditions at the area's headquarters on Butler Island. Recent topographic maps, a compass, and a pioneer spirit will also aid the visitor. The necessary transportation arrangements to Lewis Island are a small price to pay for the opportunity to observe a rare virgin forest.

Butler Island was owned and developed by Irish-born Pierce Butler, who was responsible for the introduction of the rice culture into Georgia in the late 18th century. With the help of several thousand slaves, he carved out the forests and marshes to create a rice plantation here. Butler's grandson, Pierce Neese Butler, began management of Butler Island in 1838, accompanied by his bride, the English actress Fanny Kemble. During her brief stay on the plantation Fanny Kemble wrote a Journal of a Residence on a Georgian Plantation, 1838-39, a book which became quite controversial during the outset of the Civil War.

The original dikes of the rice fields are still used, and the rice shucking plant and sugar cane mill are still standing. Butler Island has changed ownership several times since the Civil War, and in 1954 the State of Georgia obtained the property.

The waterfowl area is best enjoyed by the individual who is interested in a "fend for yourself" natural environment. Nearby Hofwyl-Broadfield Plantation and Fort King George do have facilities for the visitor seeking historical information and guided tours. Several miles into the waterfowl area is Two-Way Fish Camp, a commercial establishment that offers camper hook-ups, a boat lift, bait and tackle, a snack bar, and other items that offer aid and comfort to the modern-day naturalist, fisherman, and hunter.

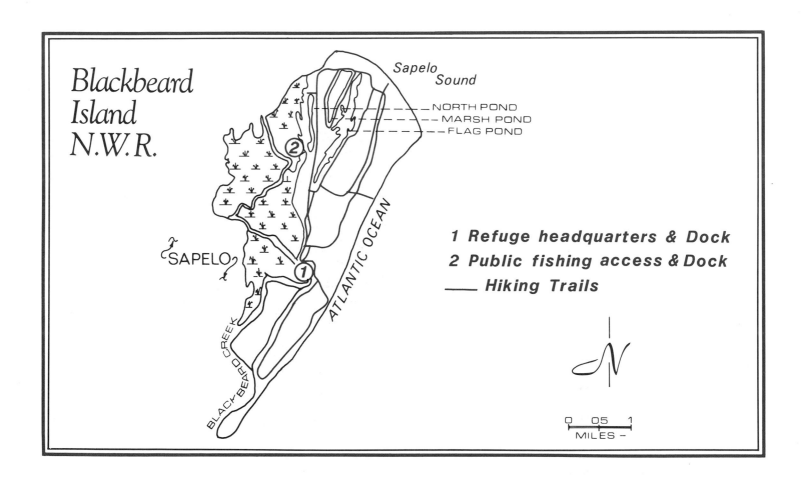

Blackbeard
Island
N.W.R.

Sapelo Sound

NORTH POND
MARSH POND
FLAG POND

ATLANTIC OCEAN

SAPELO

BLACKBEARD CREEK

1 Refuge headquarters & Dock
2 Public fishing access & Dock
___ Hiking Trails

N

0   0.5   1
MILES

Also located within the Altamaha River Waterfowl Area is Champney River Park. On the south bank of the Champney River adjacent to U.S. Hwy. 17, the park has a 2-½ acre public parking area, a fishing catwalk, and two public boat ramps. One of the boat ramps is on the Champney River, an estuary in the Altamaha delta; the other smaller ramp provides access to a 50-acre freshwater lake. The park provides access to Lewis Island and is just north of Two-Way Fish Camp and Hofwyl-Broadfield Plantation, approximately 2 miles south of Darien.

The Altamaha River Waterfowl Area is at its best when visited in the fall, winter, and early spring.

BLACKBEARD ISLAND
NATIONAL WILDLIFE REFUGE — 20

Blackbeard Island National Wildlife Refuge
U.S. Fish & Wildlife Service
Savannah Coastal Refuges
P. O. Box 8487
Savannah, GA 31412
telephone 912/944-4415

Facilities
* *boat facilities, dock only for loading and unloading passengers, or fishing*
* *brochures*
* *exhibit shelter*
* *pets on leash only*
* *picnic area*
* *restrooms*
* *tours*
* *trails*

Hours of Operation
Sunrise to sunset daily; closed two weeks annually for deer hunts in fall and winter. Portions of Blackbeard's beach may be closed seasonally to prevent disturbance to nesting, wintering, or migrating birds.

Reservations
Required to arrange tours for organized groups

Blackbeard Island is as rich in history as it is in natural resources. This barrier island, named because its thick woods and meandering creeks provided hiding places for pirates, remains remote with access only by boat. But, for the naturalist, fisherman, and beach-lover, this spot is delightful and well worth the effort to get there.

Blackbeard Island is made up of a series of roughly parallel sand dunes, each of which was the shoreline of the island at one time. In between the sand dunes are savannas, or grassy plains.

Directions
Located 18 miles east of Shellman's Bluff (Julienton River) in McIntosh County, the refuge is bordered on the east by the Atlantic Ocean, and on the west by Sapelo Island.

Some are large enough to contain water and the Fish & Wildlife Service has created many freshwater ponds which serve as habitat for innumerable birds. These ponds also contain vast numbers of alligators, which are most obvious in Flag Pond during summer months.

There are no motorized vehicles allowed on Blackbeard Island. Unravaged by swarms of visitors, Blackbeard remains clean and virtually untouched.

As a National Wildlife Refuge, the island now offers a variety of recreational opportunities year-round. Blackbeard's beach is open to the public during daylight hours for swimming and exploring the beach. The seven miles of beach are shining sand, carpeted with shells and driftwood. Wildlife observation, especially bird-watching, is excellent at all times. The beach is always alluring, since pelicans, gulls and terns can usually be seen. A variety of migrating shorebirds might also be observed skimming along the shore and diving for unwary fish. In winter months, great numbers of scaup can be seen from the beach along with several species of scooters and other pelagics. Rarities such as bald eagles and peregrine falcons are occasionally spotted soaring over the beach or perched in trees along the dune line.

In summer the loggerhead turtles make their ponderous way onto the shore to nest and leave their eggs. When possible, the researcher living on the island will review this nesting program with visiting groups and provide a tour of the hatchery. For this, special arrangements must be made.

During the fishing season (March 15-October 25), freshwater fishing is permitted on North Pond and Flag Pond. Fishing in the saltwater creeks, which cut through refuge marshlands, is always permitted. Fishermen should come prepared with bait and tackle.

The forest contains more than 20 miles of dirt trails suitable for nature walks. Live oaks, slash pine, cabbage palmettos, American holly and Southern magnolia trees prevail and are the woodland home of doves, owls, cuckoos, swifts, swallows, hummingbirds, woodpeckers, titmice, and wrens. The island is a paradise for the photographer, birder, or hiker.

The refuge provides an excellent example of a barrier island in a state of evolution, with erosion on the north end of the beach and accretion on the south end. Thus, it serves as an ideal site for beach ecology studies.

Blackbeard Island has been in government ownership since 1800 when it was acquired by the Navy Department at public auction to serve as a source of live oak timber for shipbuilding. In 1924, it was placed under the jurisdiction of the Bureau of Biological Survey, an organization which later became the U.S. Fish & Wildlife Service, as a preserve and breeding ground for native birds. In 1940, by Presidential Proclamation, Blackbeard Island Reservation was designated as Blackbeard Island National Wildlife Refuge.

From 1830 to 1900, a yellow fever quarantine station was maintained on the island under the jurisdiction of the National Board of Health. The facility, which included a tent camp hospital, was located on the south end of the island. The only remains of the station are found on the north end and include a brick oven believed to be a sulphur furnace. Sulphur gas was used to disinfect the quarantine station crew from contamination and to fumigate vessels moored off the north end of the island while cargo and passengers were unloaded.

A visit to Blackbeard promises the unique opportunity to experience an undeveloped barrier island influenced by natural forces. Families with children can enjoy swimming, exploring the beach, and nature studies. Several picnic tables and a shelter are situated near the main government dock on Blackbeard Creek, which can be reached at all tides. A small floating dock used primarily by fishermen, is located adjacent to north pond, but refer to navigational charts for important directions.

Facilities
- *boat facilities
launch*

Directions
Exit I-95 at exit #10. Turn right onto GA. Hwy. 251. Proceed 2.9 miles and turn left at the fork, leaving GA. Hwy. 251. Proceed over railroad track and take the first dirt road to the left. Proceed 5.4 miles to the end of the road — the site of Fort Barrington. Do not turn left at the East Side Fishing Camp.

**Fort Barrington, The Road to
McIntosh County Welcome Center
P. O. Box 1497
Darien, GA 31305
telephone 912/437-6684**

The sand ridge community is one of the more unusual natural communities in coastal Georgia, and the road to Fort Barrington offers the visitor a convenient opportunity to explore many features of the sand ridge.

Sand ridges in coastal Georgia are largely confined to the northern or eastern borders of some rivers, such as here on the banks of the Altamaha River. Other examples may be seen at the Savannah Science Museum's Ogeechee River property and along the Ohoopee River near Swainsboro. These sand ridges are believed to be the result of the rise and fall of sea levels, river and marine currents, and wind. The result, dramatically exhibited on the road to Fort Barrington, is a ridge of deep sand, rising as high as seventy feet above sea level and sixty feet above the adjacent Altamaha River.

This deep sand is nutrient-poor and holds little moisture for plants. Ground fires also frequently sweep through this type of community. As a consequence the plants that exist on the sand ridges are tolerant of inhospitable conditions. Many of the plants are stunted or gnarled or their leaves are thick and leatherly, all adaptions to a harsh environment. Turkey oak and longleaf pine are the predominant trees, although post oak, bluejack oak, and mockernut hickory are also present.

Southwest of the road to Fort Barrington is the river swamp of the Altamaha with its characteristic bald cypress and tupelo. To the northeast of the road, there is a less frequently flooded bay forest (loblolly bay, sweetbay magnolia, and redbay), while the pine flatwoods are on higher elevations.

Near the margins of this sand ridge, Royal Botanist John Bartram discovered what has become known as the "lost Franklinia" in 1765. This beautiful, flowering tree was last seen growing in the wild in the early 1800's. Fortunately, Bartram's collection of seeds was successfully propagated; it is from his stock that all living Franklinias are now descended.

Today's traveler on the road to Fort Barrington will see little of historic interest. However, this road, the fort, and the nearby shallow ford across the Altamaha were indeed historically significant, especially during colonial times. Scottish Highlanders, living in nearby Darien, marched along this road in 1742, part of their overland route to Fort Frederica. Continued Spanish and Indian marauding as well as the fear of French intrusion down the Altamaha, prompted the citizens of Darien to petition for the construction of a new fort. By 1762, a square fort 75 feet on each side was constructed, along with a perimeter bastion of mounded earth. The fort, named in honor of Lt. Col. Josiah Barrington, was garrisoned with 25 rangers. The soldiers patrolled colonial borders and chased runaway slaves. The site, guarding the river crossing and the overland trail between St. Augustine and Savannah, was also strategically important during the Revolutionary War, the War of 1812, and the Civil War.

There is nothing left of the wooden fort, and the meanderings of the Altamaha have eroded all but two of the fort's outer walls. The construction of a boat launching ramp through the middle of the fort has also done considerable damage to the site's integrity.

Visitors to the area should be careful to stay on the sand road. The road margins can be soft and the adjacent land is privately owned and posted. The area should particularly be avoided during the hunting season. For approximate hunting season dates, contact the McIntosh County Welcome Center.

About 3/4 of a mile east of Fort Barrington is a road turnoff to Barrington Park, a community park operated by the McIntosh County Commission. While there are no hookups, recreational vehicle or tent camping is permitted. Picnic tables, trash containers, and a boat launching ramp are provided. This makes a pleasant stop for lunch, perhaps part of a longer excursion that includes other nearby sites such as Fort King George, Hofwyl-Broadfield Plantation, and the Altamaha River Waterfowl Area.

FORT KING GEORGE — 22

Fort King George
Georgia Department of Natural Resources
P. O. Box 711
Darien, GA 31305
telephone 912/437-4770

Facilities
- *brochures*
- *demonstrations, by prior arrangement*
- *exhibits*
- *interpretive program*
- *museum*
- *pets on leash only*
- *picnic area*
- *restored fort & blockhouse*
- *restrooms*
- *soft drink machine*
- *special events/programs*
- *tours, guided by prior arrangement*
- *trail, marked*

Hours of Operation
9:00 a.m. - 5:00 p.m. Tuesday - Saturday, 2:00 p.m. - 5:30 p.m. Sunday; closed Mondays (excluding legal holidays), Thanksgiving, and Christmas Day

Admission Fee
$1.00 adults, $ .50 children age 6-12 yrs.; group fees for 15 or more, $ .75 adults, $ .25 children

Fort King George, located on the outskirts of Darien east of U.S. Hwy. 17, combines a rich history with a well-kept natural setting. The museum offers an excellent 20-minute slide show, exhibits, and artifacts, that help the visitor visualize the site's dramatic past. The walking-tour booklet, available in the museum, provides a self-guided tour and is an invaluable aid in appreciating the evolution of events here.

In 1988, a joint venture of the Georgia Department of Natural Resources and the Lower Altamaha Historical Society funded the reconstruction of the massive four-story cypress blockhouse of the fort. The fort's moat, palisades and breastworks also have been restored. The view from the blockhouse lookout window gives the visitor a panoramic view of the Altamaha Delta and distant barrier islands.

The Guale (pronounced wah-lee) Indians, native inhabitants of coastal Georgia, maintained a village here on the bluff of the Altamaha River. In 1565, Spain sent missionaries to seek Indian converts. Both Indians and Spanish priests fled English raiders in 1670. In the early 1700's, the English built the fort in an effort to counteract French expansion, and their departure was followed by commercial sawmill operations that spanned the 19th century and

Reservations
Required for group rates

Directions
Exit I-95 at exit #10. Proceed east to Darien on U.S. Hwy. 17. At Darien turn onto Spur 25 and drive 1.2 miles east to the fort.

lasted until 1926. The foundation of an old sawmill still stands. The timber exported from Darien was cut in the interior and rafted as logs down the Oconee, Ocmulgee, Ohoopee, and the Altamaha Rivers. During the era of rice growing and timber harvesting, Darien was the largest port in Georgia, and the Darien Bank was the predominant financial institution of the state.

In addition to a well-marked walking tour, there is an unmarked marsh trail of about one mile that is currently being developed. A mixture of giant Southern wildrice and brackish marsh, which is the intermediate marsh between salt marsh and fresh water, is in evidence here. Picnic tables are in the rear of the building, situated among beautiful live oaks with a lovely view of the Altamaha River.

There are special programs, such as the living history presentations, for which advance arrangements are required. But the museum personnel will arrange additional demonstrations, slides, and lectures with even one day's notice. Interpretive tours are given for large groups with advance notice.

Also a short distance from the fort are ballast-stone islands. The islands are the result of an accumulation of ballast stones that were used to stabilize the hulls of two- and three-masted schooners. These ships came to the mouth of the Altamaha River between Sapelo and St. Simon's Island and anchored temporarily. The crew would throw the ballast stones overboard before the schooner continued on to Darien to pick up longleaf pine timber, eventually creating these islands. While longleaf pine is not in evidence at Fort King George, the various stages of commercial pine forest are visible between Fort Barrington and Fort King George.

When this fort was originally built in 1721, it was guarding the main channel of the Altamaha. Over a period of about 270 years the river has changed its course significantly. Fort King George is now on a small tidal creek. The combination of a beautiful setting and an area rich in history provides equal enjoyment to the history buff or the family on a picnic.

Facilities
- *boat facilities*
  - *charter services*
- *brochures*
- *exhibits, Marine Extension Center*
- *Interpretive / educational programs being developed at the Marine Extension Center*

Hours of Operation
Open year-round

Directions
17.5 nautical miles east of Sapelo Island (buoy at 31 degrees 24.00' N, 80 degrees 52.14' W).

GRAY'S REEF NATIONAL MARINE SANCTUARY — 23
(Sapelo Live Bottom)

Gray's Reef National Marine Sanctuary
Marine and Estuarine Management Division
Office of Ocean and Coastal Resources Management
National Oceanic and Atmospheric Administration
U.S. Department of Commerce
Washington, DC 20235
telephone 202/673-5126

Marine Extension Service
P. O. Box 13687
Savannah, GA 31416
telephone 912/356-2496

Gray's Reef is Georgia's only marine sanctuary and will have special appeal to divers, fishermen, and those hoping to glimpse some of the diverse marine life that live near the reef. The sanctuary is designed to prevent destruction to the reef and to regulate fishing and other possible activities centered around the reef. The reef was named for Milton "Sam" Gray, a marine biologist and collector who first discovered the area and surveyed its flora and fauna.

Located offshore on Georgia's continental shelf, Gray's Reef National Marine Sanctuary, also known as Sapelo Live Bottom, is 17.5 nautical miles east of Sapelo Island, at an average depth of 60 feet. The sanctuary protects an elevated limestone outcrop formation that supports a rich marine-life community. The sanctuary boundaries (see recent navigational charts) encompass 17 square miles containing a system of live bottom or reef outcrops in the otherwise sandy shelf environment of the South Atlantic outer continental shelf.

Nearly all of the rock surfaces are covered with a carpet of living sponges, sea squirts, anemones, soft and hard corals, hydroids, and other organisms. Many species of crab, shrimp, and other crustaceans live within the area and support a diverse community of fishes including bass, grouper, and colorful tropicals. Pelagic predators such as barracuda, amberjack, cobia, king mackerel, and Spanish mackerel frequent the area in search of the schooling bait fish that congregate near the reef. An illustrated field guide to the fish is expected to be produced by the Marine and Estuarine Management Division.

Loggerhead sea turtles are not uncommon at the reef especially in winter when they may be found resting under ledges. The endangered right whale has recently been found to bear its young off the southeast coast and has been observed in the vicinity.

Sport fishing, scuba diving, monitoring studies and scientific research are the principal activities at the sanctuary. Prohibited activities at the reef include using destructive vessel-towed sampling devices; using wire fish traps; taking or damaging any bottom formation, marine invertebrate or marine plant; and dumping non-approved materials.

Marine sanctuaries like Gray's Reef are areas set aside by the federal government for protection and management and are under the jurisdiction of the National Oceanic and Atmospheric Administration (NOAA). Education and interpretive programs are provided by the Marine Extension Center of the University of Georgia. The center houses a marine aquarium, displays, and exhibits describing the reef and its marine life.

Access to the sanctuary is by private or chartered vessels from marinas along the coast, or trips sponsored by local dive shops. Sea conditions, visibility, and currents are variable; therefore, scuba divers should plan to dive here only with experienced supervision or advice. Fishermen should consult federal fishing regulations in the Fishery Conservation Zone of the southeast coast regarding minimum lengths for grouper, snapper, bass, Spanish mackerel, and cobia.

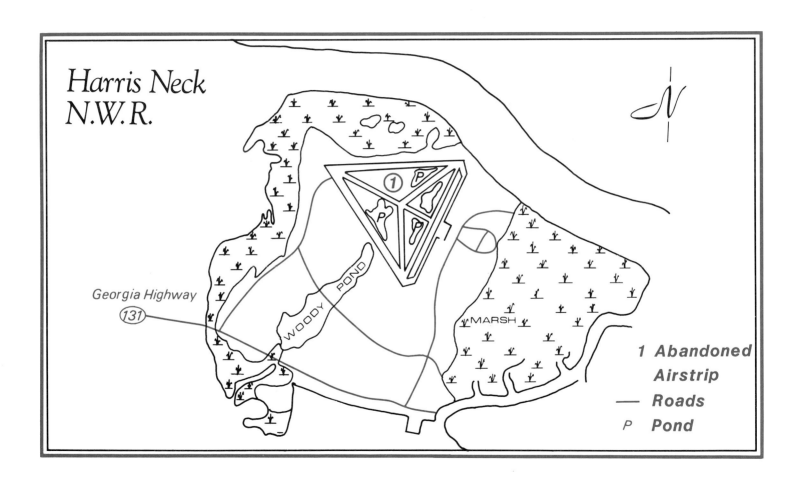

Harris Neck
N.W.R.

Georgia Highway
131

WOODY POND

1

P

P

P

MARSH

1 Abandoned
  Airstrip
— Roads
P Pond

Gray's Reef does not compare to tropical coral reefs in terms of water clarity and topographic complexity; however, the quantity of marine life here during the summer months may exceed that of coral reefs. A trip to the reef even by non-divers will undoubtedly provide a variety of experiences that may include observations of sea birds, porpoises, sharks, schooling fish, jellyfish, sea turtles, or even a whale.

HARRIS NECK NATIONAL WILDLIFE REFUGE — 24

Harris Neck National Wildlife Refuge
U.S. Fish & Wildlife Service
Savannah Coastal Refuges
P. O. Box 8487
Savannah, GA 31412
telephone 912/944-4415

Harris Neck National Wildlife Refuge, situated approximately 50 miles south of Savannah, is a rather small refuge but contains a great diversity of habitats, and hence a variety of plants and animals. Established by federal land transfer in 1962, the area was formerly managed as a World War II army airfield.

There are no formal environmental education sites, but opportunities abound for the naturalist to view a variety of land types and wildlife. The bird life is especially visible in the area. During the spring and fall migrations, the woodlands attract many species of songbirds. During the spring and summer, nesting egrets and herons are abundant in the freshwater impoundments. In the fall and winter these same areas attract hundreds of wintering ducks, particularly dabblers. Botanists will enjoy the numerous prickly pear cacti which bloom in profusion

Facilities
- boat facilities
    launch, for use at high tide, only
- exhibit shelter
- handicapped access, limited
- pets on leash only
- restrooms
- trails, marked

Hours of Operation
Fenced portions of the refuge are open Monday - Friday, sunrise to sunset; Harris Neck Creek Recreation Area is open daily during daylight hours; Barbour River Landing is open daily from 4:00 a.m. to midnight.

Directions
Exit I-95 at exit #12. Take U.S. Hwy. 17 one mile south to GA Hwy. 131. Proceed on GA. Hwy. 131 east for 7 miles to the refuge gate.

in May and June. Magnificent live oak trees also enhance this refuge, which supports a variety of hardwoods typical of the Georgia coastal plain region.

Opportunities to photograph bird life are extensive. The freshwater pools are especially popular since some type of wildlife can almost always be found here. Also, sightings of deer, armadillos, and many birds are possible while walking along the refuge road network.

Restrooms are available, but there is no provision for drinking water, and the closest convenience store is off I-95 at the South Newport River exit. A paved and marked road provides easy access so visitors can enjoy observing wildlife from the comfort of a vehicle. Also, the paved roads could be used by visitors confined to wheelchairs. The refuge is an excellent outdoor classroom where science students can study wildlife with relative ease. School groups, including those transported in schoolbuses, can tour the refuge easily since the road system can support large vehicles.

A public boat ramp, usable at high tide only, is at the refuge's Harris Neck Creek entrance on GA Hwy. 131, but few visitors use this facility. However, two fishing piers at this site are very popular. An additional public boat ramp, located on the Barbour River, provides all-tide access to nearby Sapelo Sound. The Barbour River Landing is open daily from 4:00 a.m. to midnight.

Although the refuge is open year-round, public use is low except at the Harris Neck Recreation Area on Highway 131. Guided tours are occasionally provided to conservation-oriented organizations. Arrangements for these special tours must be made at least two weeks in advance.

HOFWYL·BROADFIELD PLANTATION — 25

Hofwyl·Broadfield Plantation
Georgia Department of Natural Resources
Route 10, Box 83
Brunswick, GA 31520
telephone 912/264-9263

The traveler stopping at Hofwyl-Broadfield Plantation just south of Darien can feel the drama of the river plantations that flourished along the South Carolina and Georgia lowlands over a century and a half ago. The setting is the great Altamaha River delta, its streams and marshlands, and forests of massive moss-hung live oaks, saw palmettos, wax myrtle, and Southern magnolia trees.

The visitor center provides programs about the very large rice plantations and how they operated. The owners of these plantations worked extremely hard, made fortunes, and lived daily on the brink of ruin. A whim of tide or weather could wipe out a plantation in a matter of hours; years of invested money, time, planning, engineering, and effort would be lost.

Life on a river plantation is portrayed through a 14-minute slide program, a stroll through the museum, and referral to the well-written brochures offered at the center. The visitor may then set forth on the trail walks, informed about the things he will see.

A walk along the well-marked trail offers a glimpse of what rice cultivation must have entailed. Dikes, artificial high land constructed by slaves for use when the fields were flooded; slave-built canals for irrigation and transportation; and natural swamp habitat offer the trekker a wide variety of natural and historical viewing. Freshwater wetlands, once a virgin bald cypress swamp, and canals are filled with waterfowl and other wildlife.

The plantation house itself, albeit no "Tara," is a testimony to the Southern plantation life of many years past and has been open to the public since 1979. The history and the natural environment surrounding the Hofwyl-Broadfield Plantation are equally worthy of description.

Facilities
- *brochures and list of bird species*
- *exhibit*
- *handicapped access*
- *interpretive program*
- *museum*
- *pets on leash only*
- *picnic area*
- *restrooms*
- *soft drink machine*
- *special events/programs*
- *tour*
- *trails, marked*
- *visitor contact station*

Hours of Operation
9:00 a.m. - 5:00 p.m. Tuesday - Saturday, 2:00 p.m. - 5:30 p.m. Sunday; closed Mondays (excluding federal holidays), Thanksgiving and Christmas Day

Admission Fee
$1.50 adults, $ .75 children age 6-12 yrs., special group fees for 15 or more

Reservations
Required for group rates

Directions
Exit I-95 at exit #9. Proceed east on GA Hwy. 99, following signs, 1 mile, to the site.

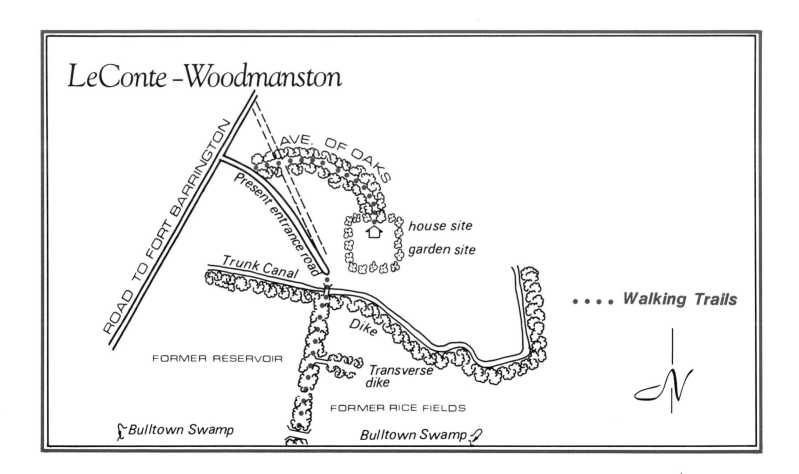

LeConte-Woodmanston

ROAD TO FORT BARRINGTON

AVE. OF OAKS

Present entrance road

house site

garden site

Trunk Canal

Dike

FORMER RESERVOIR

Transverse dike

FORMER RICE FIELDS

Bulltown Swamp

Bulltown Swamp

.... *Walking Trails*

N

Indeed, the story of one is an integral part of the other's tale. A trip to Hofwyl-Broadfield Plantation will enhance the visitor's knowledge and appreciation of coastal Georgia.

LECONTE-WOODMANSTON PLANTATION — 26

LeConte-Woodmanston Plantation
P. O. Box 356
Hinesville, GA 31313
telephone 912/884-5837 (Midway Museum), tours: 912/368-7002

LeConte-Woodmanston, owned by The Garden Club of Georgia, is a 63.8-acre historic site, formerly part of Woodmanston Plantation. Located about an hour south of Savannah, this site offers a variety of opportunities for the naturalist or botanist to explore, including a walk along a dike beside old rice fields allowed to revert to a bald cypress swamp.

LeConte-Woodmanston was acquired in 1760 by William and John Eatton LeConte, grandsons of a French Huguenot who had sought refuge from European persecution in New Rochelle, New York. Louis LeConte, son of John LeConte, assumed full responsibility for this rice plantation in 1810 and created a one-acre floral and botanical garden of international renown.

Mr. Alexander Gordon, an Englishman who visited the garden, wrote of Dr. LeConte's outstanding camellias and bulbs. The LeContes cherished and grew unusual native plants and imported many exotic plants. The LeConte pear, a cross between the sand pear and the common dessert pear, was brought to Woodmanston Plantation by Louis LeConte's brother. The hybrid pear was grown extensively for commercial use and continues to be cultivated in Georgia.

Facilities
- *brochures for self-guided tours at Midway Museum*
- *guide, volunteer available by prior arrangement*
- *trail, marked*
- *visitor center (Midway Museum)*

Hours of Operation
Open year-round

Reservations
Required to arrange tours

Directions
From the north - exit I-95 at exit #14 and drive south on U.S. Hwy. 17 for 12.5 miles past the Midway Church. Turn right at the historic marker, then take an immediate left. Continue south for 5.8 miles, and turn left at the next historic marker. Follow signs to the LeConte-Woodmanston parking area.
From the south - exit I-95 at exit #12 and drive north on U.S. Hwy. 17 for 3.7 miles. Turn left on Sandy Run Road. Drive 4.3 miles and turn left onto the dirt road. Drive 1 mile south to historic marker. Follow signs to parking area for LeConte-Woodmanston.

The Civil War left Woodmanston in sad disrepair. By this time the two sons of Louis LeConte, John and Joseph, had moved to California where John became the first president of the University of California at Berkeley, and Joseph became a distinguished professor. Joseph LeConte later participated in the founding of the Sierra Club.

Through years of neglect, the buildings of Woodmanston Plantation disappeared. The once famous gardens became overgrown as the land reverted to forest, and the rice fields reverted to bald cypress swamps. Pulpwood was cultivated at this site until 1977, when The Nature Conservancy, through the gift of the C. B. Jones Estate and Brunswick Pulp and Paper Company, donated the former residence, botanical gardens, and old rice fields to the Garden Club of Georgia. The historic value of this site was recognized by its inclusion in the National Register of Historic Sites on June 18, 1973.

Bird watchers will be pleased with the quantity of bird life present at the site, including the elusive LeConte's sparrow which was named for Major John LeConte.

The Garden Club of Georgia is still in the early stages of developing a replica of this botanical and floral garden. Further plans include a parking area, outline planting of the home site, and a presentation of the rice-growing operation. LeConte-Woodmanston should become a place of beauty and significance as well as a living memorial to the LeConte family.

LITTLE ST. SIMONS ISLAND — 27

Little St. Simons Island
P. O. Box 1078
St. Simons Island, GA 31522
telephone 912/638-7472

Facilities
- boat facilities
    docking, limited
- brochures and lists of bird and plant species
- day trips (Wednesday & Saturday)
- demonstrations
- exhibits
- food and beverage
- interpretive program
- lodging
    available only by prior arrangement
- special events/programs
- study sites
- swimming pool
- tours, guided
- trails, marked

Hours of Operation
Reservations accepted for weekends or a week

Admission Fee
Information on reservations and fees is available upon inquiry by mail.

Directions
Transportation by boat from St. Simons Island is arranged with reservations.

Privately owned, Little St. Simons is one of Georgia's best kept secrets. Located northeast of St. Simons Island, this small but diverse island is a paradise for bird watchers and nature lovers. Boats to Little St. Simons leave from the north end of St. Simons Island, and the boat ride takes approximately 20 minutes. The lodge is comfortably rustic in accommodations, and guests will enjoy picnics on the beach, horseback rides, fishing, exploring the beach, canoe trips through tidal creeks and interior freshwater ponds, guided nature trails, and just rocking on the porch of the lodge.

The 10,000-acre island boasts a long history with its most famous owners being Pierce Butler, once the owner of Butler Island located in the Altamaha River Waterfowl Area, and his actress-wife, Fanny Kemble. Pierce Butler and Fanny Kemble never actually lived on Little St. Simons, but in her book, Journal of a Residence on a Georgian Plantation, 1838-39, Fanny Kemble describes her day trips to Little St. Simons, complete with horse and carriage barged over by slaves. Rice was the main crop grown during plantation days, and use of the flooding tidal waters of the bordering Altamaha River brought in the necessary nutrients and freshwater needed to grow the cash crop. Once slavery was outlawed, the plantation system failed, and the island was left to nature once again.

Little St. Simons Island encompasses all the different coastal habitats in a very small area, allowing visitors to enjoy this diversity in a short time. Because of its habitat diversity, Little St. Simons is perhaps the best birding area on the Georgia coast. Such rare species as Wilson's plovers, least terns, and black-necked stilts nest on its beaches and in its upper dunes. The chachalaca (imported in the 1920's) is still thriving here and delights guests with its raucous rattle in the spring when the Carolina laurel cherry trees fruit in the compound yard. Guests

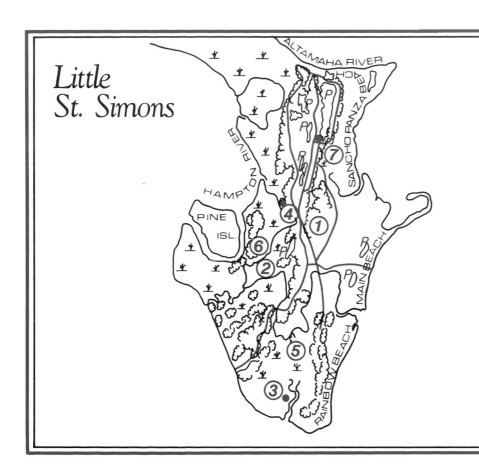

Little
St. Simons

1 **Deer Pen**

2 **Pasture Strip**

3 **Bungalow**

4 **Lodge**

5 **Nina's Hammock**

6 **Pine Hammock**

7 **East Myrtles**

—— **Roads**

P **Pond**

● **Artesian Wells**

0   1/2   1
MILES –

are also treated to the beauty of the graceful white and spotted fallow deer (also 1920's imports), and to observing the last of the ruling reptiles, the age-old alligator.

Little St. Simons is the last family-owned barrier island on the Georgia coast and has been open to the public since 1976. Limited to 20 to 25 overnight guests, visitors will experience the lifestyle of the original accommodations, which the present owners have enjoyed since 1906. Families, couples, and individuals who want to get back to nature comfortably will enjoy the remote island flavor of Little St. Simons. Easy access, general family appeal, and a wide variety of activities make Little St. Simons a one-of-a-kind treasure among resorts.

MIDWAY — 28

Midway Museum
P. O. Box 195
Midway, GA 31320
telephone 912/884-5837

Just 30 miles south of Savannah, history buffs will especially enjoy Midway's historical significance, which began with the establishment of the Midway Society in 1754. The members were dedicated to creating a church-oriented society in which Christianity and daily living were closely interrelated. During the two years that it took to complete St. John's Parish, the settlers who had arrived from Dorchester, South Carolina worked hard at cultivating rice, indigo, and other crops. The original church was destroyed by the British during the Revolutionary War; however, the present church was built in 1792 and is quite interesting to see. The key to the church may be borrowed from the museum.

The Midway Museum, situated next door, is actually a replica of an 18th century raised-cottage style house typical of the area. Those dedicated to preserving the heritage of the early settlers

Facilities
- *brochures*
- *demonstrations*
- *exhibits*
- *interpretive program*
- *museum*
- *restrooms*
- *tours*

Hours of Operation
Museum: 10:00 a.m. - 4:00 p.m. Tuesday - Saturday, 2:00 p.m. - 4:00 p.m. Sunday; closed Mondays and all holidays

Admission Fee
Museum: $2.00 adults, $1.00 students, ½ price for prearranged groups

Reservations
Advisable for groups

Directions
Exit I-95 at exit #13. Turn right and proceed on U.S. Hwy. 82 and GA Hwy. 38 to Midway.

of Georgia have done an excellent job of furnishing and maintaining the museum. Filled with antique furniture, the museum also boasts one of eight known sets in the world of musical glasses that were popular instruments in the 18th and 19th centuries. Be sure to ask the docent to play these musical glasses. There is also a slideshow documenting the history of Midway. It is shown to groups only with prior notice. Also within the museum is a small library available to anyone who wants to research the area or trace his or her genealogy. Books may not be removed from the library, but some books are available for purchase.

Across the street is the old Midway cemetery. The cemetery is always open to the public and is remarkably well preserved. Huge live oak trees shade the cemetery and add to the historical setting. Obtaining headstone rubbings by getting an impression from the headstone onto paper is permitted. A monument in the center of the cemetery honors Button Gwinnett, George Walton, and Lyman Hall, all signers of the Declaration of Independence from Georgia and all residents of this area. Midway and nearby Walthourville were also the homes of the Jones family whose mid-19th century correspondence was the subject of the award-winning Children of Pride, a vivid account of the times before and during the Civil War.

A short 5-minute ride from the museum is Hall's Knoll. This plantation homesite was the residence of physician, planter, statesman, and champion-of-freedom, Dr. Lyman Hall. An ancient live oak tree dominates the site, since the original homesite was burned in 1782 by the British. The knoll was recently donated to the Liberty County Historical Society. The society has initiated plans to maintain Hall's Knoll as a public, natural preserve. There is a Georgia Historical Commission marker at the intersection of the plantation road and U.S. Hwy. 17 to inform motorists of the knoll's historical significance.

It is unfortunate that wars repeatedly devastated Midway to the extent that recovery was finally abandoned. However, Midway today is a lovely setting boasting giant live oak trees and historical treasures.

ST. CATHERINES ISLAND — 29

Reservations
For more information contact
The Georgia Conservancy
912/897-6462

St. Catherines Island, offering a rich blend of past and recent history, is owned and managed by the St. Catherines Island Foundation with only very limited visitation allowed. This magnificent 14,000 acre barrier island hosts a survival center for endangered species, established in 1968 in cooperation with the New York Zoological Society.

St. Catherines has proven to be very hospitable to rare and endangered animals from several continents. Breeding colonies of lemurs, gazelles, hartebeests, parrots, cockatoos, and Madagascar turtles have been established and are helping to keep these nearly extinct species in viable populations.

In geologic history, St. Catherines presents a striking contrast between the older Pleistocene epoch and the more recent Holocene epoch. The older part of the island is forested with lush, subtropical vegetation; the seaward land and 11 miles of beautiful beach represent the newer development of this barrier island. These two epochs meet at the north end of St. Catherines Island in a dramatic bluff rising 22 feet over the broad, sandy beach. No other island on the Georgia coast exhibits this outstanding formation where old meets new.

The human history is no less impressive than the island's geologic history. For several thousand years a succession of coastal Indians inhabited this bountiful island. For the Guale Indians, St. Catherines was the capitol of their nation. In 1982, archaeologists discovered the 16th century Spanish mission Santa Catalina de Guale. Through this important find, scientists under the direction of Dr. David Thomas from the American Museum of Natural History are piecing together a clearer picture of the Guale Indians and their century-long coexistence with the Spanish.

Button Gwinnett, one of three Georgia signers of the Declaration of Independence, purchased St. Catherines in 1765. The historic family house in which he lived is still in use today. Slave cabins built around 1800 are also still standing. Just after the Civil War, General Sherman created an independent state for freed slaves, consisting of all the sea islands from Charleston south to the St. Johns River in Florida. St. Catherines Island became the "capitol" of this separatist state governed by Tunis Campbell. Congress repealed Sherman's directive several years later.

For all of St. Catherines' enticement and intrigue, it is difficult for the general public to gain access. The demanding research activities give the staff little time to attend to visitors. In addition, distracting traffic from the public can disturb the delicate balance of the endangered species project. So, for visitors who have an interest, it is possible to share accounts of the vital activities on St. Catherines Island, with the knowledge that its precious natural and historical resources are being preserved.

Sand Dollar

SAPELO ISLAND — 30
Including R. J. REYNOLDS WILDLIFE REFUGE and
SAPELO ISLAND NATIONAL ESTUARINE RESEARCH RESERVE

For tour information, reservations and tickets:
McIntosh County Welcome Center
P. O. Box 1497
Darien, GA 31305
telephone 912/437-6684

For group primitive camping information:
Georgia Department of Natural Resources
P. O. Box 15
Sapelo Island, GA 31327
telephone 912/485-2251

Facilities
- *brochures*
- *camping*
   organized groups only
   primitive
- *restrooms*
- *soft drink machines*
- *tours for groups by prior arrangement*
- *visitor contact station with displays and restrooms on mainland*

Hours of Operation
Tours 8:30 a.m. - 12:30 p.m. Wednesday, 9:00 a.m. - 1:00 p.m. Saturday, year-round; 8:30 a.m. - 12:30 p.m. Friday, June 1 - August 31; 8:30 a.m. - 3:00 p.m. last Tuesday of each month, March 1 - August 31

Admission Fee
$5.00 (includes boat fee) Note: All tickets must be obtained from the McIntosh County Welcome Center.

Reservations
Required

Sapelo Island, fourth largest of Georgia's barrier islands, offers several unique opportunities for visitors. The Georgia Department of Natural Resources conducts educational tours of this beautiful, undeveloped barrier island year-round.

Although seemingly pristine at first glance, Sapelo has been shaped by the activities of people for over 4000 years, and extensively so for the past 200 years. Abundant natural resources were utilized by many of Sapelo's inhabitants, the earliest of which were Paleo-Indians, who used the island as a hunting and fishing ground. Evidence of this early habitation includes hundreds of shell middens and a shell ring 12 feet high and 300 feet in diameter. These sites show the Indian's dependence on food such as oysters, deer, raccoon, and fish. Examples of the earliest pottery found in North America to date have been unearthed on Sapelo and are approximately 4500 years old.

Sapelo was significantly altered by Thomas Spalding, owner of the island from 1802-1851. An innovative planter, Spalding cut live oak to sell for shipbuilding, dug drainage ditches to aid agriculture, and cultivated sea island cotton, sugar cane, and rice. Using readily available

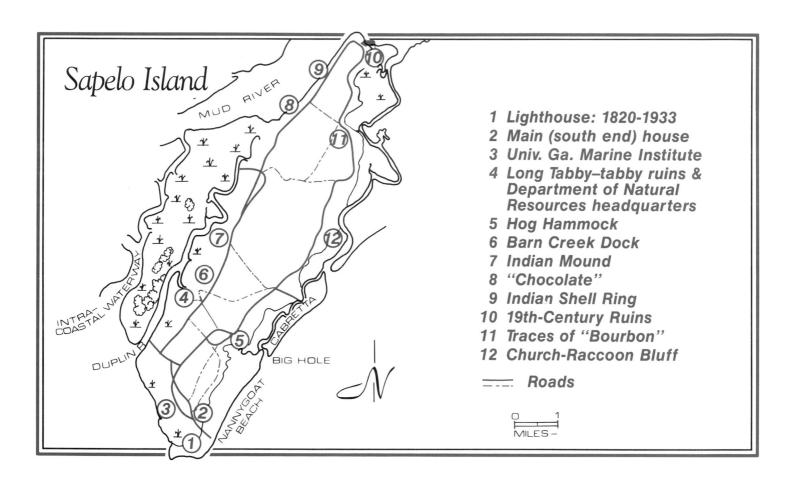

Sapelo Island

1 Lighthouse: 1820-1933
2 Main (south end) house
3 Univ. Ga. Marine Institute
4 Long Tabby–tabby ruins &
  Department of Natural
  Resources headquarters
5 Hog Hammock
6 Barn Creek Dock
7 Indian Mound
8 "Chocolate"
9 Indian Shell Ring
10 19th-Century Ruins
11 Traces of "Bourbon"
12 Church-Raccoon Bluff

--- Roads

0   1
MILES –

natural resources, he built a tabby house, which has been considerably remodeled through the years and now serves as a Conference Center for the University of Georgia Marine Institute. There are approximately 400 acres of private property on Sapelo concentrated in a community known as Hog Hammock. Hog Hammock's residents are descendants of the slaves who lived on Thomas Spalding's plantation in the early 19th century.

Howard Coffin, owner of Sapelo from 1912 to 1933, created a freshwater duck pond on the north end of the island. Paved roads and dikes were added by R. J. Reynolds of Reynolds Tobacco Company who owned Sapelo from 1933 until his death in 1965.

Current use of the island continues to modify the area. Now managed by the Georgia Department of Natural Resources, the R. J. Reynolds Wildlife Refuge is actively managed for deer and wild turkey. A timber management program is also underway. The southern tip of the island is the site of the University of Georgia Marine Institute. Established in 1953 through the invitation of R. J. Reynolds, the Marine Institute has conducted historic research in salt marsh ecology and barrier island formation. Scientists at the Institute continue this tradition of research designed to improve the understanding of coastal ecosystems.

The Sapelo Island National Estuarine Research Reserve was set aside for long-term research, education, and interpretation through the cooperative efforts of the Department of Natural Resources and the National Oceanic and Atmospheric Administration. It is one of 20 sites nationwide within the National Estuarine Research Reserve System. A primary aim of the Reserve's research and education program is to provide information to the State that is useful for decision-making concerning the development or protection of its coast and associated resources. The Reserve is sometimes referred to as the National Estuarine Sanctuary.

Today's visitors to Sapelo Island can experience a combination of barrier island ecosystems and historical modifications. On the bus tour, plants characteristic of the salt marsh can be seen, including smooth cordgrass, glasswort, salt grass, needlerush, and sea oxeye. Transition species at the marsh edge include red cedar, groundsel-tree, and marsh elder. Looking across

Directions

To the McIntosh County Welcome Center for tour tickets: exit I-95 at exit #10 and proceed east to Darien. Turn south on U.S. Hwy. 17. The welcome center is located at the foot of the Darien River Bridge on the corner of U.S. Hwy. 17 and Ft. King George Drive.

To the Sapelo Island dock: From Darien, proceed north on GA Hwy. 99 for 8 miles to Meridian. Turn right at the large "Sapelo Island Dock" sign.

the marsh visitors may see osprey feeding in the Duplin River and hear the call of the clapper rail, a common marsh bird.

Maritime forest in the R. J. Reynolds Wildlife Refuge contains live oak covered with Spanish moss and resurrection fern, laurel oak, American holly, grapevines, saw palmetto, loblolly pine, and slash pine. Also on the tour of the island, pine plantations can be seen, with evidence of timber cut as part of the Department of Natural Resources management program. Fire-scarred areas are also evident. Considered an essential part of wildlife management, controlled burning is done on various parts of the refuge. Animal species that may be seen include white-tailed deer, raccoon, feral cows, and a variety of snakes including the cottonmouth and the eastern diamondback rattlesnake. Of particular interest to birders is the presence of chachalacas, a Mexican species introduced to Sapelo as a game bird. Another spectacular summer visitor is the tiny, multi-colored painted bunting.

On the road to the beach, visitors will pass interdune meadows of wax myrtle, yucca, camphorweed, butterfly pea, and pennywort. Sapelo is alive with shorebirds and visitors can see the brown pelican feeding in the waters off the beach. The southernmost beach has a nesting colony of terns and may be off limits certain times of the year.

Sapelo can only be reached by taking a 25-minute ferryboat ride from the mainland to the island on the *Sapelo Queen*. Guides accompany visitors on a half-day bus tour, which includes a marsh walk, visits to the R. J. Reynolds Wildlife Refuge, the Sapelo Island National Estuarine Research Reserve, The University of Georgia Marine Institute, and a walk along an uncrowded beach. For those who would like a closer look, a longer tour is available March through August. Reservations are required, and all tickets for individuals or groups must be obtained from the McIntosh County Welcome Center. For educational, non-profit groups, the Department of Natural Resources also will provide transportation to a primitive group campsite.

SUNBURY HISTORIC SITE — 31

Sunbury Historic Site
Georgia Department of Natural Resources
Route 1, Box 236
Midway, GA 31320
telephone 912/884-5999

Less than one hour's drive south of Savannah is Sunbury Historic Site, a place that whets the appetite of the history buff and the naturalist. Perhaps the best way to enjoy Sunbury is with a picnic lunch under the shaded canopy of pine and oak trees overlooking picturesque marshes. It is not difficult to imagine what must have transpired on this peaceful site some two hundred years ago.

Located on a bluff overlooking the Medway River, Sunbury was a bustling port city two centuries ago and evolved into a military stronghold. Having witnessed three wars and commercial port activity significant enough to rival Savannah, Sunbury is now listed as one of the dead cities of Georgia.

The original town of Sunbury was plotted on land granted to Mark Carr by King George II in 1757. The following hundred-year period was an era of movement, wars, and change. Sunbury's fortunes changed with the times, and the town expanded into a thriving seaport and commercial center populated by wealthy planters.

In the mid-18th century Sunbury's prospects were so bright that Button Gwinnett, a signer of the Declaration of Independence and a governor of Georgia, invested in several thousand acres on St. Catherines Island, a 14,000-acre barrier island between Sunbury and the Atlantic Ocean. Sunbury's port was host to 56 vessels during 1773, while Savannah's port hosted 160 vessels.

At the same time, William Bartram, the famed naturalist, traveler, and writer from Philadelphia, discovered in and around Sunbury many of the flora and fauna the modern naturalist

Facilities
- brochures
- demonstrations
- exhibits
- guided tours
- handicapped access
- interpretive program
- museum
- pets on leash only
- picnic area
- restrooms
- special events/programs
- soft drink machines
- tours
- trails, marked
- visitor center

Hours of Operation
9:00 a.m. - 5:00 p.m. Tuesday - Saturday, 2:00 p.m. - 5:30 p.m. Sunday; closed Monday (excluding federal holidays), Christmas, and Thanksgiving

Admission Fee
$1.00 adults, $ .50 children 6-12 yrs.; groups of 15 or more - $ .75 adults, $ .25 children.

Reservations
Required for group rates

Directions
Exit I-95 at exit #13. Proceed east on GA Hwy. 38 and follow signs to Sunbury Historic Site.

will delight in today. The book of his travels devotes a number of pages to the eastern part of Georgia including nearby Colonel's Island. However, it is doubtful that the present-day visitor to Sunbury will find any "tygers," as mentioned in *Bartram's Travels*, or the huge and terrifying population of alligators that he encountered. Alligators, deer, raccoon, and opossum, however, do remain familiar sights.

By the close of the Civil War, Sunbury's bluff on the Medway River was home to fewer than a dozen families. The area's population shifted inland to take advantage of more attractive cities. The advent of the railroad inland, disease, and devastating hurricanes contributed to Sunbury's decline.

The museum and visitor center are located at the site of the old Fort Morris and War of 1812 Fort Defiance fortifications. Fort Morris was built to protect the port of Sunbury during the Revolutionary War. A few monuments in the cemetery and the earthwork of Fort Morris are Sunbury's silent reminders of the once thriving seaport. Six miles west of Sunbury is the only structure standing intact from this era. Built in 1854, the Dorchester Church is accessible from Sunbury by a quaint dirt road.

The site offers daily tours and audio-visual programs. A slide show gives the history of Fort Morris and various scenes of the area. Special programs may be arranged by writing or calling the site in advance. There are numerous brochures describing the site and surrounding area. A ranger is available to answer questions and interpret the historical and ecological aspects of Sunbury and neighboring sites in Liberty County.

Sunbury offers water enthusiasts saltwater fishing and scenic boating. A public boat ramp and a marina are within five miles of the historic site.

WOLF ISLAND NATIONAL WILDLIFE REFUGE — 32

Wolf Island National Wildlife Refuge
U.S. Fish & Wildlife Service
Savannah Coastal Refuges
P. O. Box 8487
Savannah, GA 31412
telephone 912/944-4415

Wolf Island National Wildlife Refuge, which includes Wolf Island, Egg Island, and Little Egg Island, is located in McIntosh County at the mouth of the Altamaha River near Darien. It is predominantly tidal salt marsh. Extensive stands of smooth cordgrass and needlerush are present, as well as beaches, low dunes, and small ridges of scrub cedar, wax myrtle, and pine.

The refuge offers very limited recreational opportunities and will appeal mostly to saltwater fishermen and bird watchers. Excellent tarpon and trout fishing can be found in the waters around Little Egg Island and Wolf Island. Public use in the form of exploring and picnicking is restricted primarily to the beach area.

This refuge was established in 1930. The Nature Conservancy acquired additional acreage and transferred title to the refuge system, making a total of 5,126 acres, of which only 135 acres are high ground. The refuge is home to numerous shorebirds, wading birds, and migratory waterfowl, and the beach on Wolf Island provides nesting sites for the threatened loggerhead sea turtles.

Wolf Island is a narrow strip of oceanfront beach backed by a broad band of salt marsh. Egg Island, just south of Wolf, is approximately 70 acres of scrubby brush, such as small oak and pine trees, red cedar, and dewberry. Little Egg Island contains only 10 acres and is mostly low salt marsh and sand flats. In summer months, colonies of least and royal terns nest on Little Egg Island and Wolf Island.

Facilities
- list of birds available from the Savannah Coastal Refuges' office

Hours of Operation
Sunrise until ½ hour past sunset. The refuge's beaches may be closed seasonally to prevent disturbance to nesting, wintering or migrating birds.

Directions
Located south of Sapelo Island. For complete directions, obtain the "Guide to Coastal Fishing in Georgia" for McIntosh County from the Georgia Dept. of Natural Resources, Coastal Resources Division, 1200 Glynn Avenue, Brunswick, GA 31523-9990; telephone 912/264-7218.

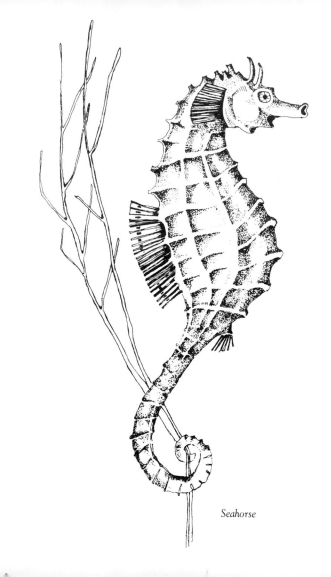

Seahorse

SOUTHERN COAST

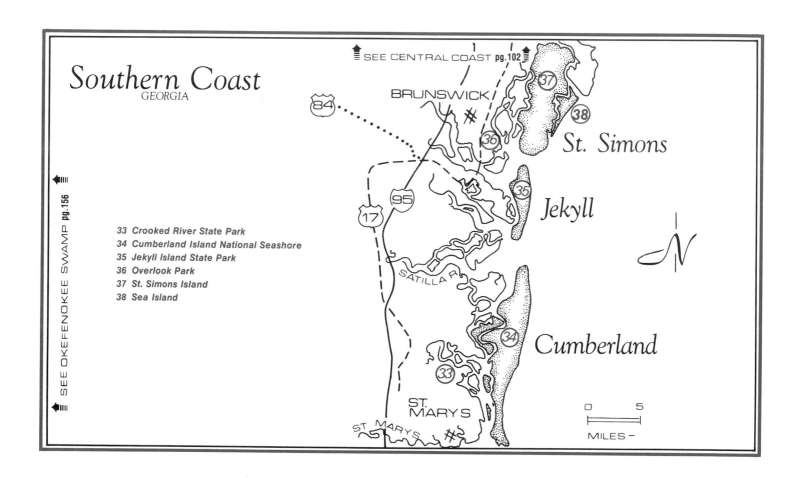

Southern Coast
GEORGIA

SEE CENTRAL COAST pg.102

BRUNSWICK

84

37

38

36

St. Simons

35

Jekyll

95

17

SATILLA R.

Cumberland

34

33

ST. MARYS

ST. MARYS

N

33 Crooked River State Park
34 Cumberland Island National Seashore
35 Jekyll Island State Park
36 Overlook Park
37 St. Simons Island
38 Sea Island

SEE OKEFENOKEE SWAMP pg.156

0   5
MILES –

CROOKED RIVER STATE PARK — 33

Crooked River State Park
Georgia Department of Natural Resources
3092 Spur 40
St. Marys, GA 31558
telephone 912/882-5256

Adjacent to the Crooked River, a tidal estuary near the historic town of St. Marys and just 11 miles from Cumberland Island National Seashore, this park offers fishing and boating opportunities. As a day trip, the visitor might enjoy hiking one or both of the nature trails to observe the plant and animal life present in the park. The careful observer might glimpse a raccoon, an armadillo, or a fox squirrel.

The hiking trail wanders for 1.5 miles through the woods past a tupelo pond. The Sempervirens Nature Trail takes the visitor for a 1/2 mile hike to the salt marsh. Along this trail is an excellent example of a sub-tropical, broadleaf forest. The trail, composed of bridges and boardwalk, is designed to protect delicate areas from too much human contact and to keep one's feet dry.

The picnic area overlooks the river, and a lucky visitor may spot an osprey or a red-tailed hawk searching for a meal. The painted bunting and eastern bluebird are warm weather visitors, and in the winter, many migrating birds stop to rest here.

Saltwater fishermen will be attracted to Crooked River State Park. A new dock has just been added from which the fishermen can cast a shrimp net, crab, or fish.

This state park is the perfect place to spend the night before visiting Cumberland Island, and the cottage or campground allow a choice in accommodations. Just 10 miles off the interstate, its proximity to I-95 also makes the park a good rest-stop to stretch tired legs or to have a picnic.

Facilities
- *boat facilities*
- *brochures*
- *camping*
  primitive
  intermediate
  recreational vehicle
- *food and beverage*
- *handicapped access, limited*
- *interpretive programs, by prior arrangement*
- *lodging*
- *pets on leash only*
- *picnic areas and shelters*
- *restrooms*
- *special events/programs*
- *swimming pool*
- *tours, guided by prior arrangement*
- *trails, marked*
- *visitor center*

Hours of Operation
7:00 a.m. - 10:00 p.m. 7 days a week, year-round

Admission Fee
Fee for camping, cottages, and pool

Reservations
Camping reservations maximum 30 days in advance; cottage reservations maximum 11 months in advance, recommend 60 days in advance

Directions
Exit I-95 at exit #2. Proceed east on GA Hwy. 40 approximately 4 miles. Turn left at Kings Bay Road. Proceed 4 miles to Kings Bay Submarine Base. Turn left at base entrance and proceed 2½ miles to park entrance.

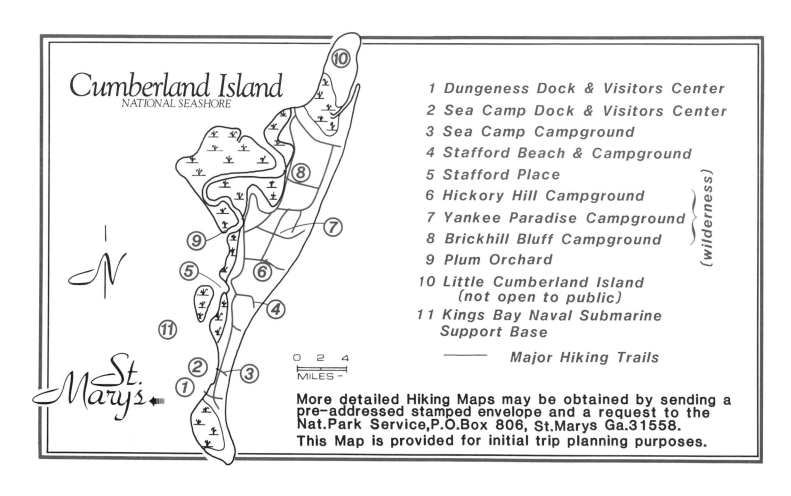

Cumberland Island
NATIONAL SEASHORE

1 Dungeness Dock & Visitors Center

2 Sea Camp Dock & Visitors Center

3 Sea Camp Campground

4 Stafford Beach & Campground

5 Stafford Place

6 Hickory Hill Campground

7 Yankee Paradise Campground

8 Brickhill Bluff Campground

9 Plum Orchard

10 Little Cumberland Island
(not open to public)

11 Kings Bay Naval Submarine
Support Base

(wilderness)

———— Major Hiking Trails

0 2 4
MILES

More detailed Hiking Maps may be obtained by sending a pre-addressed stamped envelope and a request to the Nat.Park Service,P.O.Box 806, St.Marys Ga.31558. This Map is provided for initial trip planning purposes.

N

St. Marys

CUMBERLAND ISLAND NATIONAL SEASHORE — 34

Cumberland Island National Seashore
National Park Service
P. O. Box 806
St. Marys, GA 31558
telephone 912/882-4335 (reservations), 912/882-4336 (information only)

The visitor seeking to discover one of the world's finest barrier islands will find Cumberland Island an experience of a lifetime. Undoubtedly a national treasure, Cumberland is a sixteen mile long barrier island managed by the National Park Service (NPS) as a National Seashore. By an Act of Congress in 1972, Cumberland is now protected for its outstanding scenic, historic, and natural qualities. In 1982, the northern half of the island was added to the National Wilderness Preservation System, thus ensuring the maximum protection available under federal law.

Most of Georgia's undeveloped barrier islands have a fine beach, a variety of natural communities, and a human history that spans thousands of years. Cumberland has these features, too. So what makes a visit to the island so special? Among the attributes that bring Cumberland to the top are the solitude and tranquility, the relative ease of access, the abundance and diversity of natural areas, the fascinating history, and the outstanding interpretive programs and resources.

Cumberland's solitude and tranquility are protected by strict limits on the number of people who can visit the island at any one time. At present, that limit is 300 persons per day. Further, the wilderness designation and the distances from the ferryboat docks mean that in the northern part of the island one can be alone. Sitting on the beach with the moss-draped live oaks as a backdrop, one can watch the sun rise seemingly out of the Atlantic Ocean. Looking to the north and south, the beach first becomes blurry and then disappears over the curvature of

Facilities
- boat facilities
  docking, limited
  harbor
- brochures, trail guide and list of bird species
- camping
  intermediate
  primitive
- demonstrations
- exhibits
- guided tours, by prior arrangement
- handicapped access, limited
- interpretive program
- lodging
- museum
- picnic areas
- restrooms
- rest areas
- special events/programs
- study sites
- trails, marked
- tours
- visitor contact station

Hours of Operation
8:15 a.m. - 4:30 p.m. 7 days a week, year-round, closed Christmas day; ferry departs mainland 9:00 a.m. and 11:45 a.m., and leaves the island at 10:15 a.m. and 4:45 p.m. daily, excluding Tuesdays and Wednesdays in the off-season

Admission Fee
Ferry $7.88 adults, $6.50 senior citizens, $4.01 children 12 years and under

Reservations

Required for camping and highly advisable for ferry. Reservations are taken only by telephone between the hours of 10:00 a.m. and 2:00 p.m. Telephone lines are frequently busy and callers are advised to try many times. Reservations may be made up to 11 months in advance.

Directions

Exit I-95 at exit #2. Turn east on GA Hwy. 40 and proceed to St. Marys. The National Park Service headquarters and ferryboat departure point are located on the St. Marys River waterfront in downtown St. Marys.

the earth without a building, seawall, or other manmade structure obstructing the view. The last tide may have erased all footprints but one's own.

Access to the island is by ferryboat and requires both a reservation and a fee. The NPS operates, through a concessionaire, a 150 passenger ferryboat, the *Cumberland Queen*, that transports visitors from the NPS mainland headquarters on the waterfront of St. Marys to Cumberland. The ferry stops twice at the island, at Dungeness Dock and Sea Camp. A visitor can go to the island for an afternoon or a full day. With an additional campsite reservation, one can stay overnight up to seven days.

The Greyfield Inn, a private commercial facility located about a mile and a half north of Sea Camp, operates a private ferryboat service from Fernandina Beach, Florida. Departure times, fees, room availability, and other information are available from Greyfield Inn (4 North 2nd Street, Chandlery Building, Drawer B, Fernandina Beach, Florida 32034; telephone 904/261-6408).

A very limited number of spaces are available at the Sea Camp dock for private boats to tie up. The spaces are available on a first-come, first-served basis, but it is advisable to call the NPS to let them know of an arrival.

The NPS ferryboat ride from St. Mary's takes about 45 minutes. Traveling down the St. Marys River, one may pass one of Georgia's larger shrimp fleets, home from plying the waters of the southeast coast. Soon the river sweeps through a broad expanse of salt marsh — bright green with new growth in the spring, golden brown in the fall. One will then pass the Gilman Paper Company's paper Mill and in the distance, the U.S. Navy's nuclear submarine base at Kings Bay. Closer to the island, the dorsal fins of bottlenosed dolphins momentarily emerge from below the water's surface. As the boat turns north into Cumberland Sound, the island's Beach Creek marsh comes into view. Here feral horses are often in sight. The transition to the island becomes complete with the arrival at the docks. The first stop is Dungeness Dock, and it offers easy access to the historic Dungeness area of Revolutionary War hero.

Nathanael Greene, and wealthy Thomas Carnegie. The beach is about a mile and a half away. The second stop is Sea Camp, departure point for trips into the backcountry. Sea Camp is also closer to the beach, an easy half mile away.

Cumberland's natural and historic features are both diverse and abundant. One may also take advantage of the excellent interpretive programs and displays offered by the NPS. Supplementary reading materials are available for sale in the visitor center in St. Marys.

A visit to Cumberland is a special event, and one that is worthy of the inconvenience of having to get a reservation. This procedure can be simplified, however, if plans are made well in advance. The NPS opens the reservations book eleven months in advance, and callers should be prepared to try many times before reaching an open line. Reservations may be made only by telephone or in person. Written reservation requests are not accepted. The most popular times to visit Cumberland are during the spring and fall. It is easier to get both ferryboat and campground reservations during the off-season and particularly during the winter. The visitor should be aware that the ferryboat does not operate on Tuesdays and Wednesdays during the off-season. Also, carry all gear, food, and supplies that will be needed, as there is no concessionaire on the island.

The visitor may enjoy the unspoiled beauty of Cumberland Island on this largest and southernmost barrier island of the Georgia coast, and know from the instant one's feet touch island soil, the release of tensions and mainland worries promised to the select few allowed to visit Cumberland Island.

Facilities

- *bicycle rental*
- *boat facilities*
  - *charter*
  - *dock*
  - *hoist*
  - *launch*
  - *marina*
- *brochures*
- *camping*
  - *intermediate*
  - *recreational vehicle*
- *demonstrations*
- *exhibits*
- *food and beverage*
- *fuel, ice and bait*
- *handicapped access*
- *interpretive programs*
- *lodging*
  - *hotel/motel/villas*
  - *rental property*
- *museum*
- *pets on leash only*
- *picnic areas*
- *restrooms*
- *rest areas*
- *special events/programs*
- *tennis center*
- *tours, multiple daily*
- *trails*
- *visitor contact station*
- *water park*

JEKYLL ISLAND — 35

Jekyll Island Authority
Convention & Visitors Bureau
One Beachview Drive
P. O. Box 3186
Jekyll Island, GA 31520
telephone 912/635-3636 or toll-free 800/342-1042 (within Georgia), 800/841-6586 (out-of-state)

A myriad of activities and possible accommodations await the visitor to this relatively small barrier island. Named by Oglethorpe in honor of Sir Joseph Jekyll, a financial provider for the young colony of Georgia, Jekyll Island is approximately 7 miles long and 1-1/2 miles wide. Jekyll Island offers swimming, fishing, golfing, biking, hiking, nature classes, and exploring the beach to name a few activities. Historians will find a fascinating mixture of events to ponder while exploring this island, one of Georgia's few barrier islands that is easily accessible to the public.

Like other coastal Georgia islands, Jekyll was first inhabited by Indians who used the island for hunting and fishing, and later by the Spanish in the 16th century. In the mid-18th century Oglethorpe claimed the island for the British. The colonists planted hops and grain and, according to tradition, the first brewery was established to supply Savannah and neighboring settlements with a local beer.

In 1858, after slave ships had been forbidden to land or unload their cargo on United States soil, the last slave ship, the "Wanderer," unloaded its cargo of African slaves on the beaches of Jekyll. The owners of the ship were prosecuted, and the case received national attention.

Jekyll Island was purchased in 1886 by a select group of millionaires who formed the Jekyll Island Club. The nation's wealthiest families, such as the Rockefellers, the Morgans, and the Pulitzers belonged to this club, where they hunted and golfed during the winter months. The club represented a trend among wealthy Americans to invest in Georgia barrier islands. Islands such as Cumberland, Little St. Simons, Sapelo, St. Catherines, Ossabaw, and Wassaw were purchased by single families, which ultimately led to the preservation of these islands in their natural state.

Jekyll remained the exclusive playground for the wealthy until 1947, when the island was purchased by the State of Georgia for the development of a state park. A causeway completed in 1954 allowed the public easy access to Jekyll. The Jekyll Island Club Historic District, formerly Millionaires Village, is what remains of a bygone era. It is administered by the Jekyll Island Museum. Several of the club cottages are open to the public.

Located between St. Simons Island and Cumberland Island, Jekyll Island offers the naturalist a variety of natural communities to observe. Beach, salt marsh, maritime forest, and freshwater sloughs await the explorer. Bicycles are the recommended vehicle for most visitors who wish to see the island at a relaxed pace. Native plants and wildflowers of barrier islands can be observed as well as numerous shore and wading birds, such as pelicans, terns, skimmers, herons, egrets, and oystercatchers. In the forest the quiet stalker may glimpse the elusive painted bunting or a wild turkey. To enhance these observations, *A Field Guide to Jekyll Island* can be obtained by contacting the University of Georgia Marine Extension Service in Brunswick (912/264-7268).

A highlight on Jekyll Island for those who are interested in loggerhead sea turtles is the turtle walks which are conducted by a qualified naturalist upon request by groups during the nesting season from mid-June to mid-August. The length of the walk, which hinges on seeing a loggerhead turtle, is generally 2-3 miles long, from approximately 10:00 p.m. until 11:00 p.m., and is recommended for adults. Children under 16 must be accompanied by an adult. Reservations are suggested a week in advance. For further information or reservations, contact the Recreation Office (912/635-2232).

A favorite path for bird watchers lies between Shell Road and the Ben Fortson Parkway (turn north off the Parkway onto a small road beside the gas station). The path passes through the marsh and maritime forest and crosses a wooden bridge which spans a small tidal creek.

Hours of Operation
Open year-round

Parking Fee
$1.00 toll to enter the island; fees for camping

Directions
Driving north, exit I-95 at exit #6. Proceed north on U.S. Hwy. 17. Following the signs to Jekyll Island, turn right onto the Jekyll Island Causeway.

Driving south, exit I-95 at exit #8. Proceed approximately 4.3 miles on GA Highway 25 to U.S. Highway 17. Drive south on U.S. Highway 17. Follow signs to Jekyll Island, turn left onto the Jekyll Island Causeway.

It then winds north through an oak and pine forest. The path ends at Stable Road near the Jekyll Island Club Historic District.

There are three picnic areas on the island. The north picnic area offers a view of the salt marsh. Near here is another bike path which meanders through oak and cabbage palmetto woods, and pine and cedar hammocks. This path also skirts the marsh, offering an opportunity to observe various marsh communities and wildlife. For the historian, the old duBignon burial ground is also on the northern end of the island. The duBignon family once owned Jekyll Island. Nearby, a free fishing pier offers a broad view of St. Simons Sound.

The south picnic ground, St. Andrews picnic area, is separated from the beach by huge sand dunes with a boardwalk access to the beach. Near here is a spot for bird-watching in an area which was once intended for a marina. Because of seepage and silting, the plans were abandoned, and the one-time harbor is now completely exposed at low tide. There is also a 1/4 mile footpath made of oyster shells along the Jekyll River.

South Dunes picnic area, recently renovated, includes sheltered picnic tables, as well as a large screened gazebo. A pathway between two small ponds leads to a wide cross-over that winds through the dunes to the beach.

Jekyll Island, run by the Jekyll Island Authority, is a developed barrier island with many remaining natural features. The island offers the visitor numerous recreational and educational opportunities and is easily affordable for family vacations.

OVERLOOK PARK — 36
GEORGIA DEPARTMENT OF NATURAL RESOURCES, EXHIBIT ROOM

Coastal Resources Division
Georgia Department of Natural Resources
1200 Glynn Avenue
Brunswick, GA 31523
telephone 912/264-7218

Overlook Park and Georgia Department of Natural Resources Exhibit Room provide a short stop for the visitor in the Brunswick area who is interested in a walk through the salt marsh. A small picnic area overlooks the marshes of Glynn.

The Georgia Department of Natural Resources (DNR) offers a wealth of coastal information for the visitor including numerous brochures. The brochures cover a wide variety of subjects, including how to catch, cook, and clean blue crabs, how to throw a cast net, and a beachcombing guide. The Department of Natural Resources is the primary agency charged with the protection of such coastal resources as marshlands, dunes, shrimp and fisheries, and environmental protection. The Department is planning to move to a new headquarters building at the northeast foot of the Sidney Lanier Bridge in 1990. New and expanded displays and exhibits are planned.

The boardwalk into the salt marsh extends approximately 100 feet spanning a small tidal creek. At the end of the boardwalk is a larger creek where fishing, crabbing, and shrimping are permitted. The boardwalk is always open and provides a close-up view of the changes in a saltwater creek as the tides flow in and out.

Facilities
- *brochures and lists of bird and plant species*
- *picnic tables*
- *trail, boardwalk marked*

Hours of Operation
Park: daily, year-round; Coastal Resources Division: 8:00 a.m. - 4:30 p.m., Monday - Friday, closed holidays

Directions
Driving south, get off I-95 at exit #8, the North Golden Isles Parkway. Proceed east for 4.3 miles to intersection with U.S. Hwy. 17. Turn right and drive 2.3 miles. Overlook Park is on the left.

Driving north, get off I-95 at exit #6, the South Golden Isles Parkway. Turn right onto parkway and proceed 9 miles. Overlook Park is on the right.

- *bicycle rental*
- *brochures*
- *boat facilities*
    docking
    harbor
    launch
    marina
- *charter services*
- *food and beverage*
- *handicapped access*
- *interpretive programs*
- *lodging*
    motel/hotel
    rental property
- *museum*
- *pets on leash only*
- *picnic areas*
- *restrooms*
- *tours*
- *visitors center*

Hours of Operation
Open year-round; visitors center open 9:00 a.m. - 5:00 p.m. 7 days a week, year-round

Admission Fee
$ .35 toll for Torras Causeway.

ST. SIMONS ISLAND — 37

St. Simons Island Chamber of Commerce
Neptune Park
St. Simons Island, GA 31522
telephone 912/638-9014

St. Simons Island, one of the largest of Georgia's barrier islands, deserves several days of relaxed exploring to fully appreciate the generous and varied offerings. Although extensively developed, the island, with its abundant marshes, white sandy beaches, and spectacular live oaks, has not lost its sea island charm.

To capture the essence of the island, the naturalist might enjoy participating in one of the beach or marsh walks that are regularly scheduled from June through August. It is interesting to note that the East Beach, located near the Coast Guard station, is rapidly accreting. The beach is wide and there are well developed interdune meadows. At the north end of East Beach, at Gould's Inlet, this sandy plain opens into an extensive shoal system. A variety of shorebirds may be spotted here, particularly during the warmer months of the year, including the brown pelican, black skimmer, and a variety of gulls, terns, and sandpipers.

For the more adventurous, there is a trail which begins at the intersection of Frederica Road and the causeway to Sea Island. This path is essentially a horse trail through high marsh, but it is possible to park the car on the edge of the road and hike through the woods to the marshlands.

Neptune Park at the south end of the island is located beside the pier in the village. Picnic facilities are plentiful, and there is a nice view of St. Simons Sound. The park provides easy access to the beach for exploring or bird-watching, and children will find the playground an extra bonus.

St. Simons is one of the few islands on Georgia's coast where community life has been predominant. The Creek Indians had more than one settlement on the island, and the Spanish had three missions here during the 16th century, one of which was named San Simon, but they were abandoned by the 1680's.

In 1736, Oglethorpe established an English settlement on the island to defend English landholdings from the Spanish. Fort Frederica, named for Frederick, Prince of Wales, became a walled and moated fortress on the island's west side. Fort St. Simons was established at the south end of the island in the same general area as the present-day lighthouse and pier.

In a surprise attack in 1742, the British, aided by Creek Indians and Scottish Highlanders, defeated the Spanish on St. Simons Island in the Battle of Bloody Marsh. The remaining Spanish returned to St. Augustine, and military reinforcements were no longer necessary to protect the colonists from the Spanish.

After the Revolutionary War, landholders on St. Simons began to cultivate sea island cotton, and quite a few prosperous plantations contributed to the active community life.

During the Civil War the island was evacuated, and when landholders returned, they quickly realized that life would never again be the same. Over the years many of the old plantation tracts have been subdivided into neighborhoods, country clubs, and small resort communities.

Today, St. Simons is thriving with many permanent residents and year-round tourists, but it still retains a natural beauty that can be appreciated by all. Whether you come to play golf or tennis, to fish, to explore the beaches, or to bird-watch, the pleasing climate of St. Simons can offer something for everyone.

Nestled in the natural beauty of the island are several historic sites worth visiting. The most notable are listed below, but other spots to see include the U.S. Coast Guard Station, which has special group tours (call 912/638-3319), the Arthur J. Moore Methodist Museum at Epworth-by-the-Sea, the Tabby Slave Cabin, Massengale Park, and Mallery Park.

Directions

Driving south, exit I-95 at exit #8. Proceed approximately 4.3 miles on GA Hwy. 25 to U.S. Hwy. 17. Drive south on U.S. Hwy. 17 for 1½ miles. Turn left onto Torras Causeway.

Driving north, exit I-95 at exit #6. Proceed north on U.S. Hwy. 17. After crossing the Sydney Lanier Bridge, follow signs for St. Simons Island. Turn right onto Torras Causeway.

Facilities
- *bookstore*
- *brochures*
- *exhibits*
- *museum*

Hours of Operation
10:00 a.m. - 5:00 p.m. Tuesday - Saturday, 1:30 p.m. - 5:00 p.m. Sunday, Memorial Day - Labor Day; 1:00 p.m. - 4:00 p.m. Tuesday - Saturday, 1:30 p.m. - 4:00 p.m. Sunday, Labor Day - Memorial Day; closed Mondays, Christmas, New Years, Good Friday and Thanksgiving.

Admission Fee
Museum and lighthouse: $1.50 adults, $1.00 children 6-12 yrs.

Directions
After crossing the Torras Causeway, bear right and follow Kings Way to the second traffic light. Continue to the next caution light and turn right. Proceed to the lighthouse and adjacent museum.

St. Simons Lighthouse and the Museum of Coastal History

Coastal Georgia Historical Society
101 12th Street
St. Simons Island, GA 31522
telephone 912/638-4666

Museum of Coastal History
P. O. Box 1136
St. Simons Island, GA 31522

Islands and lighthouses seem to go together, and St. Simons Island has one of two lighthouses on the Georgia coast open to the public. From the lighthouse, the view of St. Simons Inlet, Jekyll Island, and the Atlantic Ocean is the best anywhere, and on a clear day it is well worth the climb.

The original lighthouse was destroyed in 1862 by the retreating Confederate Army. In 1872, a new lighthouse was built with an adjacent keeper's cottage. These were designed by a famous Georgia architect, Charles Cluskey. The Coast Guard now maintains the facility as one of the nation's oldest continuously working lighthouses, while the museum operates tours.

The Museum of Coastal History is in the old lighthouse keeper's cottage and houses changing exhibits and other historical artifacts from coastal Georgia's history. The nine-room house, constructed of Savannah grey brick, has Georgia heart pine floors. The complex is on the National Register of Historic Places.

Christz Church, Frederica

This beautiful church is the second oldest Episcopal Church in Georgia and the third oldest church in the state. Cruciform in design, Christ Church embodies island charm, serenity, and warmth. The giant virgin live oaks which surround the church are inspirational and demand a reverent approach to this site.

The present church was consecrated in 1886 after the original was destroyed in the Civil War. Christ Church was rebuilt by the Reverend Anson Green Phelps Dodge, Jr., who became the central character in Eugenia Price's The Beloved Invader, the first book of her trilogy on St. Simons Island. Other volumes in the trilogy are The Lighthouse and New Moon Rising. The interior of the church is all wooden with a trussed gothic roof. The crowning glory is the series of magnificent stained-glass windows.

A quiet walk through the graveyard where many of the early settlers are buried is a step back into history. Some of the gravestones bear names of many of the historic characters written about by Eugenia Price.

Facilities
- brochures
- handicapped access

Hours of Operation
2:00 p.m. - 5:00 p.m. daily summer, 1:00 p.m. - 4:00 p.m. daily winter.

Admission Fee
Donation requested

Directions
Drive north on Frederica Road 4¾ miles. The church is on the left just past the Lawrence Road fork.

Fort Frederica National Monument

National Park Service
Route 9, Box 286-C
St. Simons Island, GA 31522
telephone 912/638-3639

Overlooking the marsh and the Frederica River, Fort Frederica is the site of St. Simon's first English settlement. Established in 1736 by James Edward Oglethorpe, Frederica was a self-sufficient community of about 500 soldiers and citizens with shops and small businesses. Its

Facilities
- brochures
- demonstrations June 15 through Labor Day; by prior arrangement the rest of the year
- exhibits
- handicapped access
- interpretive programs June 15 through Labor Day; by prior arrangement the rest of the year
- museum
- pets on leash only

- restrooms
- soft drink machine
- special events/programs
- tours, by prior arrangement

Hours of Operation
9:00 a.m. - 6:00 p.m. daily, June 15 through
Labor Day; 9:00 a.m. - 5:00 p.m. daily, Labor
Day until June 15; closed Christmas

Admission Fee
$1.00 for ages 17-61, ages 16 and under and 62
and over free.

Directions
Fort Frederica: Drive north on Frederica Rd. 5
miles from Demere Road (¼ mile north of Christ
Church).

Bloody Marsh Battle Site: Follow signs to the
site of the marsh off Demere Road, east of
Frederica Road.

major purpose was to defend the colony from the Spanish, and the historian will find much of interest in reading diagrams and listening to taped dialogue which creates the real atmosphere of pre-revolutionary Georgia.

In the museum, the visitor can pick up a brochure for a self-guided tour and view exhibits dealing with the archaeological excavation of this village. Outside, tabby ruins of the old fort and well-marked outlines of the old town can be seen, as well as part of the original moat which surrounded the fort. While enjoying the wide expanse of trees, flowers, and shrubs overlooking the marshlands, one may hear the raucous call of a pileated woodpecker high in the massive oaks, or see an osprey soaring over the river.

The visitor may also want to take a moment to note the natural destruction which threatens this historic site. Ruins are deteriorating, and erosion has claimed 50 percent of the original bank along the river. The bank was recently covered with a wire mesh and planted with cordgrass in an effort to counter the effects.

An integral part of Fort Frederica's history is the Battle of Bloody Marsh. The site of the battle has been preserved by the National Park Service and is just a short drive away from Fort Frederica. There is ample parking at the battle site. The visitor will want to listen to a pre-recorded message, approximately three minutes long, under the small covered shelter. There are beautiful live oak trees here overlooking an excellent view of the salt marsh.

SEA ISLAND — 38

Sea Island Company
Sea Island, GA 31561
telephone 912/638-3611

Facilities
- *lodging*
  hotel
  rental property
- *brochures*

Sea Island is a resort established in 1927 by auto magnate Howard Coffin. The island is privately overseen by the Sea Island Company, and home rentals may be secured through the company. Otherwise, the general public is not allowed access to the beach on this barrier island, and only the roads are open.

Residents of private homes and guests of The Cloister®, a resort hotel on Sea Island, may enjoy the island. The Cloister® offers guided nature tours of the island and other neighboring islands. A Sea Island field guide is also available through the Sea Island Company.

Ancient live oaks covered with resurrection fern are most notable, and the back of the island is on a saltwater tidal creek which separates Sea Island from St. Simons Island. But, for the most part, the vegetation in the residential and hotel areas on Sea Island is a carefully manicured combination of native and introduced species. A number of plants were chosen for use because they are evergreen.

For those who are boating in the vicinity or staying in Sea Island accommodations, the best bird-watching to observe royal and Caspian terns, avocets, pelicans, cormorants, and migratory shorebirds is at Pelican Spit on the northern end of the island at the mouth of the Hampton River. At the end of the main road, Pelican Spit is off the beach to the northeast, and binoculars or a spotting scope would be helpful.

Hermit Crabs

OKEFENOKEE SWAMP AREA

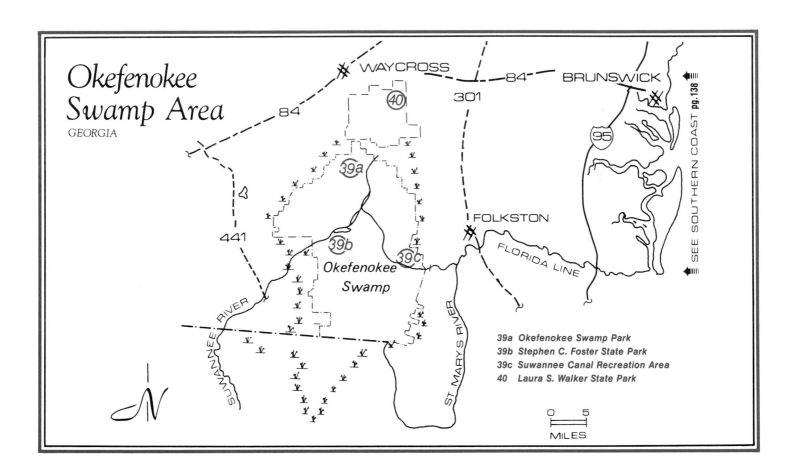

Okefenokee
Swamp Area

GEORGIA

WAYCROSS

84

BRUNSWICK

301

40

39a

441

FOLKSTON

FLORIDA LINE

SEE SOUTHERN COAST pg.138

95

39b

Okefenokee
Swamp

39c

39a Okefenokee Swamp Park
39b Stephen C. Foster State Park
39c Suwannee Canal Recreation Area
40   Laura S. Walker State Park

SUWANNEE RIVER

ST MARYS RIVER

N

0   5
MILES

OKEFENOKEE SWAMP — 39

Okefenokee National Wildlife Refuge
U.S. Fish & Wildlife Service
Route 2, Box 338
Folkston, GA 31537
telephone 912/496-7836

The Okefenokee Swamp is internationally renowned as one of the largest and most ecologically intact swamps in North America. It is a fascinating, alluring place that may appear forbidding to the uninitiated, but in reality it is one of the earth's special places to experience beauty, tranquility and mystery. Its black waters mirror majestic and awe-inspiring scenes. Each explorer is captivated and intrigued by the mosaic of vegetation: vast open prairies, scrub forests, towering bald cypress, and tupelo stands. A profusion of wildflowers, blooming from early spring to late fall, and an abundance of animal life add to the experience. A memorable adventure awaits those who wish to enjoy this unique wilderness.

The Okefenokee Swamp encompasses 423,721 acres of southeastern Georgia with a few acres in the northeastern corner of Florida. Some 70 to 90 percent of the water entering the swamp comes from rainfall. What water is not lost to evaporation is discharged into both the Suwanee River and the St. Marys River. The Okefenokee is itself the sluggish headwaters for these two rivers, but only in certain places is the current evident to the visitor.

The word Okefenokee is an Indian term meaning "land of the trembling earth." The term accurately describes the principal feature of most of the land masses in the swamp. New vegetation grows faster than the old can decompose, producing deep layers of peat on top of the ancient sand that was once the ocean floor. Methane gas is produced by the decomposing layers of peat; this gas forces great masses or "batteries" of peat to break away from the bottom of the swamp and float to the surface. Grasses, shrubs and eventually trees become established on these batteries, and a new island is formed. The island is anchored somewhat by roots, but it may shake as one steps on it, hence the name trembling earth.

The swamp is not a uniform environment; it is made up of open water, prairies, shrub, and forest. If left totally undisturbed, the swamp's vegetation would eventually change through a process called succession to become cypress forest.

Fire is a frequent phenomenon in the swamp, due primarily to lightning. Occurring during periods of drought and low water, fires prevent the vegetation from reaching its natural climax condition. Most of the fires are of low intensity, but occasional hot fires will consume enough of the peat to return the area to its original condition: open water. The most recent major fire occurred in 1954. Evidence of it, including charred tree trunks, may still be seen on the east and west side of the swamp.

Human association with the Okefenokee goes back at least 4000 years. Indian inhabitance in the Okefenokee Swamp dates back as early as 2000 B.C. Over 25 mound-villages were built in the vicinity of the swamp between 500 B.C. and 1000 A.D. Small bands of Timucuan Indians inhabited the swamp from 1550 to 1700. In the 18th and 19th century, the Okefenokee became a refuge for Indians displaced from their homelands. Around 1820, Chief Billy Bowlegs led his Seminole band into the swamp to escape the encroaching white settlers. From the safety of the swamp, he led raids on nearby settlements. In 1838, General Charles Floyd was ordered to stop Chief Billy and his warriors. General Floyd penetrated the swamp, but never found his quarry. Chief Billy then led his band south to the ultimate safety of the Florida Everglades. Two of the swamp's largest islands pay tribute to the pursuer and the pursued - Floyd's Island and Billy's Island.

By the late 19th century, proposals were advanced to drain the swamp for agricultural purposes and to harvest the timber in the process. Captain Harry Jackson and his Suwannee Canal Company obtained permission from the Georgia legislature to dig a canal into the swamp. The canal was started on the eastern side of the swamp at Camp Cornelia (now the Suwannee Canal Recreation Area) in 1891. It was about 40 feet wide and six feet deep. After a 13-mile long canal was dug, the drainage project was abandoned, and the company subsequently failed in 1897.

By 1909, the Hebard Lumber Company had acquired much of the swampland, and after a careful planning effort, proceeded to harvest timber. By 1927, when it ceased operations, the company had removed over 1/2 billion cubic yards of timber, most of it cypress. A latticework of rail and tram lines scarred the swamp. The Hebard Lumber Company did not clear cut the swamp and left trees standing that were not economical to harvest. Consequently, there are still some virgin tracts in the swamp. On the northeastern side of Grand Prairie, there are some cypress trees whose estimated ages are as much as 587 years.

As the Hebard Lumber Company was running out of timber to harvest, efforts grew to protect the swamp. One of the leaders of this drive, Mrs. Francis Harper, wrote to President Franklin Roosevelt, a personal friend, conveying her fears for the Okefenokee if it were not preserved by the government. On March 30, 1937, President Roosevelt established the area as a refuge, later named the Okefenokee National Wildlife Refuge. The refuge encompasses 396,315 acres, including most of the swamp and some adjacent uplands. Further protection was provided by Congress when, in 1974, most of the refuge was added to the National Wilderness Preservation System.

The swamp can be enjoyed in different ways, either from the comfort of a guided motorboat or from a wooden walkway constructed above the waters of the swamp. Personal boats are permitted within the swamp provided the motor's horsepower is less than 10. Outboard motors can be rented at two of the swamp's entrances. The best way to experience the swamp is by canoe, for some trails, due to the area's wilderness status, are not open to motorboats. Canoeists can spend from one to four nights in the swamp camping on wooden platforms which can accommodate groups of from 2 to 20.

There are three primary entrances to the Okefenokee, and each offers a dramatically different encounter, with the swamp. For convenience, these access points are described separately.

No matter how one experiences the swamp, the adventure promises to be exciting and rewarding. Georgia's Okefenokee Swamp is a unique wilderness and a gem that can fortunately be enjoyed by all.

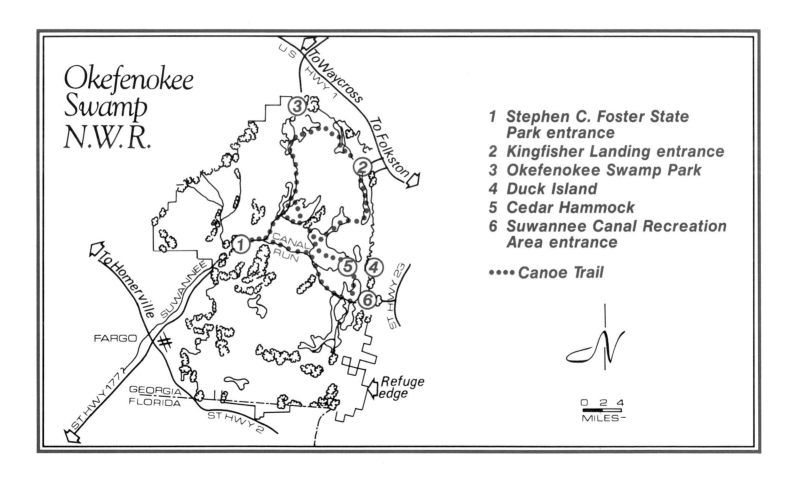

Okefenokee Swamp N.W.R.

1 Stephen C. Foster State Park entrance
2 Kingfisher Landing entrance
3 Okefenokee Swamp Park
4 Duck Island
5 Cedar Hammock
6 Suwannee Canal Recreation Area entrance

•••• Canoe Trail

OKEFENOKEE SWAMP PARK — 39a

Okefenokee Swamp Park, Inc.
Waycross, GA 31501
telephone 912/283-0583

On the northern perimeter of the Okefenokee is the Okefenokee Swamp Park. Access through this park provides what may best be described as a managed experience. One does not need to be a stouthearted adventurer to come here. Yet, in a few hours, a visitor will become introduced to the swamp and with some of the animals inhabiting this wilderness.

The initial visitor contact point contains a small store selling a wide range of souvenirs. There are restrooms, vending machines, and a place to purchase tickets for entry into the park.

The Okefenokee Swamp Park, a non-profit development, offers the visitor a lengthy boardwalk into the swamp at the end of which is a 90-foot observation tower. The price of admission also includes a 20-minute guided motorboat tour through some of the waterways, wildlife lectures, films, exhibits of live bears and deer (seen from air-conditioned observation rooms), a pioneer exhibit commemorating an 1838 Indian massacre, and of course many large alligators.

The swamp here consists mainly of young cypress and tupelo. It offers neither the spectacle of towering trees that one finds near the western entrance to the swamp (Stephen C. Foster State Park) nor the vast open prairies of the eastern side (Suwannee Canal Recreation Area). But it is convenient, and ones does not need to make elaborate or careful plans to participate in the swamp experience through the Okefenokee Swamp Park.

There are no overnight facilities at this entrance, but Laura S. Walker State Park is located only a few miles to the north. The city of Waycross is also nearby, offering motels, restaurants and other facilities.

Facilities
- *boat tours*
- *brochures*
- *canoe rental*
- *food and beverages*
- *interpretive programs*
- *museum*
- *pets must be secured on a leash not to exceed six feet in length; however, not advisable to bring pets since the entire swamp is habitat for alligators*
- *picnic areas, tables and pavillion for groups*
- *rest areas*
- *restrooms*
- *special events*
- *study sites*
- *trails, marked*
- *visitor contact station*

Hours of Operation
9:00 a.m. - 6:30 p.m. 7 days a week spring and summer; 9:00 a.m. - 5:30 p.m. 7 days a week fall and winter

Admission Fee
$7.00 adults, $6.00 senior citizens 62 and over, $5.00 children ages 6-11 yrs., $6.00 per person for groups

Reservations
Required for groups

Directions
Exit I-95 at exit #6. Proceed on U.S. Hwy. 84 west toward Waycross. At the intersection with GA Hwy. 177, turn left and proceed 11 miles to the park entrance.

Facilities
- *boat facilities*
- *brochures and lists of wildlife species*
- *cabins*
- *camping*
    - *primitive*
    - *intermediate*
    - *recreational vehicle*
- *canoe trails and rentals*
- *exhibits*
- *handicapped access*
- *pets - must be secured on a leash not to exceed six feet in length; however, not advisable to bring pets since the entire swamp is habitat for alligators*
- *picnic area*
- *rest areas*
- *restrooms*
- *special events/programs*
- *tours*
- *trails, marked walking and canoe*

Hours of Operation
6:30 a.m. - 8:30 p.m. 7 days a week, March 1 - Labor Day; 7:00 a.m. - 7:00 p.m. 7 days a week, Labor Day to February 28

Reservations
Advisable for cabins, sometimes needed for campsites

Directions
Exit I-95 at exit #6, and proceed to Waycross on U.S. Hwy. 84. Continue west on U.S. Hwy. 84 to Homerville. Turn left onto U.S. Hwy. 441 south and proceed to Fargo. At the intersection of GA Hwy. 177 turn left and proceed to the park.

STEPHEN C. FOSTER STATE PARK — 39b

Stephen C. Foster State Park
Georgia Department of Natural Resources
Route 1
Fargo, GA 31631
telephone 912/637-5274

On the western side of the swamp, near the town of Fargo, a gradually curving peninsula of high ground penetrates the depths of the Okefenokee. At its end is the Stephen C. Foster State Park. Departing from here by canoe the visitor will soon see some of the large bald cypress trees and open waters characteristic of the swamp. A short canoe ride will bring the paddler to Billy's Island, once the town site supporting the Hebard Lumber Company's operations. Another excursion takes the visitor to Minnie's Lake. Still another leads to the Suwannee River Sill, an earthen dam built after the 1954 fire and designed to maintain high water levels year-round in the western portion of the swamp.

The state park offers a variety of services, ranging from guided motorboat tours to rental boats, outboard motors, and canoes which can be rented overnight. There is a small store with limited supplies of food, beverages, and fishing gear. Picnic shelters, campgrounds, rental cabins, nature trails, and an interpretive center are also provided.

One can depart from Stephen Foster on several canoe trails. However, advance reservations are necessary to secure rental canoes and to camp in the swamp overnight. Trail reservations, information, and regulations should be obtained from the U. S. Fish & Wildlife Service.

SUWANNEE CANAL RECREATION AREA — 39c

Suwannee Canal Recreation Area
U.S. Fish & Wildlife Service
Okefenokee National Wildlife Refuge
Route 2, Box 338
Folkston, GA 31537
telephone 912/496-3331

On the eastern side of the Okefenokee, the prairies are extensive. Open waters, scrub forests, and tall bald cypress trees are also there. In the judgment of many, this entrance offers the most to the visitor with limited time. The Suwannee Canal Recreation Area is located approximately 11 miles southwest of Folkston, and also has a boardwalk which ends in a 35-foot high tower that affords a panoramic view of the prairies, bald cypress domes, and a lake. There are self-guided nature trails for the visitor to leisurely walk and observe birds and plants. The prairies are the best location for sighting the Florida sandhill crane. Also of interest is the Chesser Island Homestead, the authentic homesite of the Chesser family for almost 100 years. The concessionaire at the recreation area rents canoes and motorboats and offers guided tours by boat down the Suwannee Canal. This entrance to the swamp is only 35 miles from I-95.

The Suwannee Canal Recreation Area is the departure point for two of the canoe trails into the swamp. Others originate at Kingfisher Landing, 12 miles north of Folkston, or Stephen C. Foster State Park, but arrangements, such as permits, must be obtained through the U.S. Fish & Wildlife Service office. Reservations can be made up to two months in advance.

These canoe trails lead across the swamp to Stephen C. Foster State Park or they loop back to the point of origin. Trips ranging in length from two to five days are available on a reservation basis. Guided overnight canoe trips are available from licensed outfitters. Names of outfitters can be obtained through the U.S. Fish & Wildlife Service.

Facilities
- *bicycle rental*
- *boat facilities and rentals*
- *boat tours*
- *brochures and lists of wildlife species*
- *canoe rental, shuttle, and guided expeditions*
- *exhibits*
- *food and beverage*
- *handicapped access*
- *interpretive programs*
- *pets must be secured on a leash not to exceed six feet in length; however, not advisable to bring pets since the entire swamp is habitat for alligators*
- *picnic areas*
- *restrooms*
- *special events/programs*
- *study sites*
- *trails*
- *visitor contact station*

Hours of Operation
8:00 a.m. - 6:00 p.m. Monday - Friday, September 11 - February 29; 7:00 a.m. - 7:30 p.m. Saturday and Sunday, March 1 - September 10; closed Christmas Day

Reservations
Advisable for groups, boat tours with guides, and rentals; c/o Concessionaire, Suwannee Canal Recreation Area, Folkston, GA 31537; telephone 912/496-7156

Directions
Exit I-95 at exit #2. Proceed on GA Hwy. 40 west to Folkston. Turn onto GA Hwys. 23/121 south and proceed 7 miles. Turn right onto Spur 121, and drive four miles to the recreation area.

Facilities
- brochures and list of bird species
- boat facilities
    docking
    ramp
- camping
    primitive
    intermediate
    groups
    recreational vehicle
- canoe rental
- interpretive program, by prior arrangement
- lake
- pets on leash only
- picnic area, some shelters
- restrooms
- swimming pool
- vending machines

Hours of Operation
7:00 a.m. - 10:00 p.m. 7 days a week, year-round

Admission Fee
Fee for camping and shelters

Reservations
Recommended for camping weekends, holidays and during hunting season; required for group camp and kitchen, and picnic shelter

Directions
Exit I-95 at exit #6. Proceed west on U.W. Hwy. 84 to GA Hwy. 177. Proceed on GA Hwy. 177 south for 2 miles to the park.

LAURA S. WALKER STATE PARK — 40

Laura S. Walker State Park
Georgia Department of Natural Resources
Route 6, Box 205
Waycross, GA 31501
telephone 912/283-4424

Laura S. Walker State Park, located near Waycross, Georgia, is a popular state park in south Georgia. Situated in "Okefenokee Country," the park offers a variety of activities for the recreationalist, ranging from waterskiing to camping.

Built by the Works Progress Administration (WPA), the park holds the distinction of being one of the few Georgia parks named for a woman. Mrs. Laura Singleton Walker was supporting and encouraging conservation long before it became popular to do so. Not only did she work at protecting the trees she loved so dearly, but she also was a strong community leader. This park was once part of a federal program during the depression years that was established to protect the area's natural resources. The more attractive features of the park are due largely to this program and the ongoing protection and preservation of the natural plant and animal community.

Whether you plan to visit for the day or camp for a while, the park draws outdoor enthusiasts of all ages. Swimming is permitted during the summer only when the pool is open and a lifeguard is on duty. Fishing is allowed throughout the year with a valid state fishing license. A fishing dock and boat launching area are provided. Although private boats are allowed, be sure to check with the park office concerning boating hours.

Several types of camping facilities are provided. There is little privacy, but the amenities are present, including 44 combination tent and trailer sites. During the hunting season, this area fills up very quickly. There is also an area designated for group camping, as well as a pioneer camping ground.

One particularly interesting feature at the park is the presence of a colony of red-cockaded woodpeckers. This bird is listed as an endangered species because its nesting sites are often destroyed during timber harvesting.

Whatever the activity, a visit to the park can be a fun, comfortable experience, especially if one takes the time to plan in advance. To insure a safe visit as well, review and comply with the park rules, a copy of which can be obtained at the park office.

Laura Walker State Park is located within the Dixon Memorial Forest, and provides easy access to Okefenokee Swamp Park, which is just nine miles away.

River Habitat

RIVERS

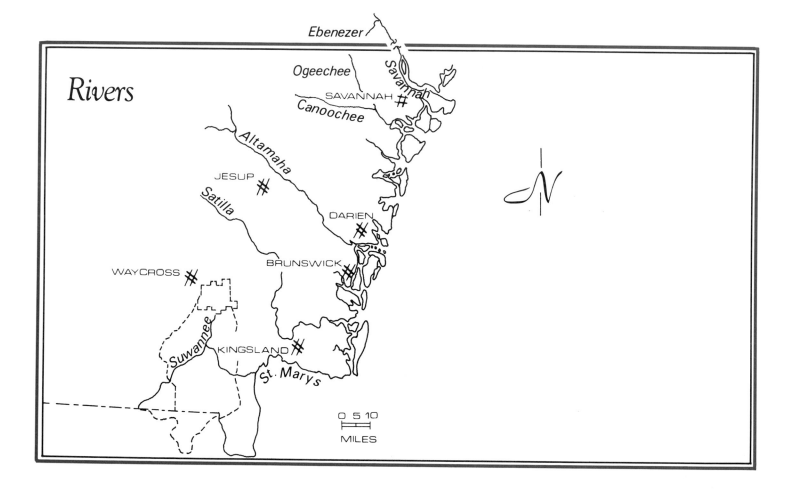

Rivers

Ebenezer

Ogeechee

Savannah

SAVANNAH #

Canoochee

Altamaha

JESUP #

Satilla

DARIEN #

WAYCROSS #

BRUNSWICK #

Suwannee

KINGSLAND #

St. Marys

N

0 5 10
MILES

INTRODUCTION TO GEORGIA'S COASTAL RIVERS

Today the rivers of coastal Georgia are a precious recreational resource. Centuries ago they represented the arteries of civilization as the principal highways for travel and transport. Rivers were also an important source of food for both the Indians and colonial settlers. Rivers were used as natural boundaries for county and state lines. Georgia is defined by the Savannah River to the north and the St. Marys River to the south.

Today, to enjoy coastal Georgia's rivers and the remote beauty and serenity they offer, a canoe is probably the best mode of transportation. The quiet of a canoe allows the paddler more occasions to glimpse wildlife on the banks of the rivers, as well as the opportunity to reflect on the history of the river before the advent of superhighways and motorboats.

Assuming the canoe will be used to visit these coastal rivers, a few suggestions might be made for maximum safety and enjoyment. By no means is this section to be considered the final authority on canoeing coastal Georgia waters. A good reference book to obtain before planning a canoe trip is Canoeing South Georgia Waters. If a motorboat is used to visit these rivers, be sure to check river water levels at the local marinas or fishing camps.

Although coastal rivers appear gentle and slow-moving, perfect for the novice, rivers are sometimes deceptive and may become dangerous under flood conditions. Water levels in the smaller, winding rivers rise rapidly following heavy rains, and today's meandering stream may be tomorrow's swift-moving current. Water levels also drop rapidly, and the short, no-portage run may require much more time and energy when there are many portages. Trees rooted in sandy banks are often washed free, resulting in submerged snags or downed trunks that span the river. Such obstacles may be at any height, inches above the stream, canoe seat high, or overhead, depending upon the river volume. Tree falls often occur in curves where the stream is actively eroding the bank and these obstacles may not be visible until the canoe is almost upon them, requiring a quick maneuver to avoid a collision. The canoeist should stay on the inside of curves to avoid this possibility.

Another facet of coastal rivers to understand is multiple river channels. When rivers are flooded, much of the water flows through the adjacent swamp forest instead of in the main channel. In some cases, a secondary channel may even form. The current here may be surprisingly swift and may "suck in" an unwary paddler.

In general, the water is swiftest during the rainy season, winter and early spring. This is also when the water is coldest. Beautiful blue skies and cold temperatures often come on the heels of winter rains. Although parties of two or more boats are always recommended, it is especially important during cold, wet seasons. Each boat should have extra wool or polypropylene clothing in a waterproof bag in case one or more boats get in trouble. Both wool and polypropylene are effective even when wet.

The canoeist should try to paddle as quietly and as far away from a fisherman's lines as possible, avoid private beaches, and should not check trot lines. On the larger rivers, speed boats are a hazard. Their wakes can easily swamp a canoe. For these rivers, an air horn is advisable.

The effect of the tides often extends upriver for a number of miles. The canoeist should take tidal flow into account and paddle with the tide rather than against it.

Especially for longer trips, it is advisable to file a trip plan with the local sheriff. If your shuttle cars are to be left in different counties, notify *both* sheriffs' departments to avoid having one's car towed away or other action.

Low-impact camping is recommended on all rivers. High ground along the river is generally private property and permission to use this land must be obtained from property owners. At moderate water levels, sandbars are favorite camp sites. The choice sites generally have some plant life growing on them, and like other sand environments these areas are relatively fragile. Piles of driftwood embedded in the sand, along with other organic materials, are good sites for developing trees and shrubs. Unfortunately, the sticks make good firewood also. If a fire is desired, wood should be gathered from the flood plain. Gas stoves are

preferable, especially since smoky fires may alarm landowners. During the spring, large parties should avoid tracking up the whole sandbar, especially if the bar is covered in part with tender young plants. Paths should be restricted to the more sterile sections of the bar.

Canoeing these ancient rivers allows the visitor to capture an essence of Georgia that is possible nowhere else. For a further discussion on the rivers, refer to the "Natural Communities of Coastal Georgia" in this guide. The visitor should enjoy the beauty of these rivers and treat them with healthy respect.

Coastal Canoe Outfitters:
- Ogeechee Canoe Outpost
  Route 4, Box 451-B
  Savannah, GA 31406
  telephone 912/748-7634

- Wilderness Outfitters
  103 Montgomery Crossroads
  Savannah, GA 31406
  telephone 912/927-2071

- Canoe Outpost, Inc.
  Route 1, Box 156
  Hilliard, FL 32046
  telephone 904/536-7929

ALTAMAHA RIVER

Just east of Lumber City, the Ocmulgee and Oconee Rivers join forces at "The Forks" to become the mighty Altamaha, and just 25 miles further the Ohoopee River adds its clear dark water to this unique major river. The Altamaha courses its way for 137 miles from middle Georgia to the coast where it unloads its voluminous sediments and deposits which become the main building materials of interior islands and barrier islands near its mouth. The Altamaha River has a wide delta and extensive river swamps along its entire length. It has no dams or impoundments and consequently is perhaps the largest, virtually unspoiled and unaltered river, complete with its river swamp, in the Southeast.

The economic importance of the Altamaha lies within its river swamps and along its banks. Towering bald cypress trees in the river swamps and pine and hardwood trees along its banks have been cut for timber since the early 1800's. Today lumbering along the Altamaha still provides the principal economic base for the region. Until the early 1900's, the Altamaha was also the main means of transporting harvested timber to the sawmills at the port of Darien. For over a hundred years giant rafts (some over 200 feet long by 100 feet wide) laden with cut timber were floated to the seaport of Darien, then loaded aboard waiting sailing vessels destined for ports around the world. Georgia hardwoods were well received because of the excellent quality of wood. When railroads were built after the Civil War, and highways were built in the 1930's, the Altamaha's role as a major lane of transport ceased.

In addition to providing timber, the Altamaha proved economically important in the growing of rice. From the late 1700's to the Civil War, rice was grown in marshes that line the river delta. Slave labor made it financially feasible, and the fact that the Altamaha is influenced by the tide for some 40 miles upriver also made conditions favorable for the cultivation of this crop. At high tide the ocean water backed up the river water, making it possible to flood the rice fields. Through a system of ditches and canals with locks, the freshwater was trapped as the outgoing tide lowered the water level. The rice industry failed when slave labor was no longer available.

Today the Altamaha provides outdoor lovers with many miles of scenic river to canoe, river swamp to experience, river islands to explore, and tidal marshes to enjoy. In August, 1978, ITT Rayonier, Inc. donated to the state 1,331 acres of land bordering the river. Because of this, canoeists and boaters are able to enjoy one of the most scenic and wild areas along the Altamaha called the "Narrows". This border of land extends 300 feet wide from the river banks located in three adjacent counties – Long, McIntosh, and Wayne. The establishment of this segment of scenic border is the first cooperative effort of its kind between individual land owners and the Georgia Department of Natural Resources.

Of the many people who have enjoyed and studied this scenic river and its environs, William Bartram is perhaps the most famous. During his travels through Georgia and other Southern coastal states from 1773 until 1776, Bartram journeyed down the Altamaha River. The plants and animals he recorded – alligators, wood storks, and other birds – can all still be seen, as well as bald cypress, wax myrtle, pine, bay, and holly. On the Altamaha near Fort Barrington, John and William Bartram found the *Franklinia alatamaha*, a small magnolia-like tree, which can no longer be found in the wild. Because Bartram took a specimen back to his garden in Philadelphia and propagated it, the species still survives and can be seen occasionally in formal gardens.

Much of the Altamaha is a wilderness river in the truest sense, and its wide channel provides the canoeist with a different experience than most Georgia rivers. The Altamaha River has limited access and the few local landings are often hard to find. To relieve the long road distances for shuttle cars, it is usually advisable to canoe a stretch of the river where put-in and take-out points are on the same side of the river. Ask directions locally or see a topographic map. Be sure to recognize the selected take-out point from the river or risk an unplanned overnight stop on the river. Canoeists that plan a trip well will be rewarded by serene wilderness paddling, excellent birding, and a chance to see the best stand of virgin cypress in the state on Lewis Island in the lower reaches of the river. The myriad of islands and the many channels in the tidal area are especially confusing and require a map and compass to navigate safely.

Suggested for an easy day's paddle at a pace of about 2.5 miles per hour:

• 11.8 miles - Paradise Park to Ft. Barrington

• 9.5 miles - Paradise Park to Lower Sansavilla
• 7.4 miles - Bethlehem Church to Paradise Park via the Penholoway Creek and Penholoway River
• 7.7 miles - Lower Sansavilla to Altamaha Park
• 9.7 miles - Highway 341 to Paradise Park via Penholoway Creek and Penholoway River

Suggested for a longer day paddle or an easy overnight paddle:

• 15.1 miles - Doctortown to Paradise Park via the Altamaha for 7.6 miles, Old River for 4 miles, and the Penholoway River or 3.5 miles
• 19.6 miles - Doctortown to Paradise Park via the Altamaha for 18.6 miles and 1 mile upstream on the Penholoway River
• 17.2 miles - Paradise Park to Altamaha Park

Suggested for longer overnights:

• 34.8 miles - Doctortown to Altamaha Park
• 29.4 miles - Doctortown to Ft. Barrington

CANOOCHEE RIVER

The Canoochee River begins as a small creek southeast of Swainsboro in Emanuel County and flows 85 miles before emptying into the Ogeechee River above King's Ferry at Interstate 95. It is joined by Fifteen Mile Creek south of Metter in Candler County and becomes almost "canoeable". A few adventurous canoeists have entered it where Georgia Highway

129 crosses between Claxton and Metter and have found mostly shallow swamps and a few deeper water stretches known locally as "lakes". When the river is high after considerable rain, it can be canoed from near the corner of Candler, Bulloch, and Evans counties, although the put-in is difficult and many deadfalls must be portaged.

Canoeing becomes possible from the good landing at Georgia Highway 169 or the next put-in where the county road, known in Claxton as Church Street, crosses the river. This section is nice because there are definite banks and only a few short portages. At the next crossing, on U.S. Highway 301 north of Claxton, the landing is the site of a small public park. Here the river flows over a sandstone outcrop known as "The Rocks," and at low water there is a miniature white water run.

Below U.S. Highway 301 the river winds alternately through avenues of arching branches of willows, Ogeechee limes, water ash, river birch, and a tangle of catbrier and ladies-ear-drop vines, or under open skies between steep banks. The next entry point is near Rogers Bridge where the Nevils-Daisy Road crosses. Visible here are a steep sand ridge on the north side and a low flood plain on river right. This combination is characteristic of little rivers and creeks that flow southeastward through the sandy coastal plain. The canoeist may see brown water snakes, often mistaken for cottonmouths, on branches over the river. A sharp slap on the water with the paddle blade will generally clear the branches of snakes so that none will drop into the canoe. Turtles, insects and small spiders are in abundance along the river. Many wasp and hornet nests hang in the willows close to the water. The paddler should avoid disturbing these nests, because the slightest provocation may bring out the angry occupants. The best refuge in such an attack may be in the water with a life jacket on, proceeding rapidly downstream with boat in tow. The paddle may also serve as a prod to poke into shallow water or into the vegetation growing at the water's edge, since cottonmouths lurk in such spots. Rattlesnakes are more likely to be on higher, drier ground above the flood plain. Occasionally, alligators find their way upstream, but most often they remain in the lower reaches.

Various species of birds, occasional squirrels, and deer may make an appearance along the banks, and tracks in the wet sand and mud attest to the presence of a variety of night creatures such as raccoons, opossums, and bobcats who also make their homes near the river. In addition, many interesting plants such as marsh mallows and spider lilies will delight any paddler who ventures down the Canoochee.

Not far above U.S. Highway 280, Lott's Creek enters the river, increasing the flow. A small park provides easy access where U.S. Highway 280 crosses west of Savannah. A short distance downstream, the Canoochee enters the Fort Stewart Military Reservation, and the prospective canoeist must obtain a special permit. Without a permit, boat and gear may be confiscated. As the river exits from the military reservation, it enters the broad Ogeechee River just above the I-95 bridge. The take-out is at King's Ferry landing on the left bank immediately below the U.S. Highway 17 bridge.

Suggested day trips:
- GA Hwy. 169 to U.S. Hwy. 301
- U.S. Hwy. 301 to Rogers Bridge on Nevils-Daisy Road
- Rogers Bridge to U.S. Hwy. 280

For trips into or through the Fort Stewart Military Reservation, check with base provost marshal's office.

EBENEZER CREEK

Only an hour's drive from Savannah, Ebenezer Creek provides several leisurely day trips for canoeists. Ebenezer Creek is the only coastal stream designated a "Wild and Scenic River" by the Georgia General Assembly and has been called "Georgia's best example of a backwater stream ecosystem" by Dr. C. H. Wharton, emeritus professor from Georgia State University. According to Dr. Wharton, the backwater condition is caused by the accumulation of sand and silt at the mouth of Ebenezer Creek where it enters the Savannah River. This sediment partially blocks the drainage of the creek, causing the water to back up, forming an elongated lake. The water level may fluctuate as much as eight feet, and it may remain high for long periods of time. The long periods of inundation may be responsible for the greatly enlarged bases of the bald cypress and tupelo tree trunks. Low nutrient availability may be responsible for the trees' dwarfed condition. The swamps bordering the creek contain excellent examples of water tupelo and virgin bald cypress swamp. Many other aquatic plants such as parrot feather, pennywort, carnivorous bladderwort, tiny duckweed, and the floating mosquito fern occur in abundance. The bald cypress and tupelo trees that line the creek are hosts to such epiphytic plants as Spanish moss, resurrection fern, the uncommon green fly orchid, and the parasitic American mistletoe.

Ebenezer Creek provides opportunities for year-round canoeing. Water levels vary drastically with the seasons and each level offers its own unique experience. Caution should be observed when the upper reaches may be too low to paddle during summer and fall. During spring flooding, the waters spill over the banks, obscuring the creek's course, making overhanging limbs a hazard. The high water of spring allows canoeing of two upper sections of the creek that are normally too low. These sections are very narrow and winding and usually require several short portages around fallen trees. However, the intimate passages, high bluffs, and abundant wildlife amply reward the persistent paddler. The lower section is particularly intriguing at these water levels, because canoeists can enjoy unlimited side excursions through the bald cypress or tupelo swamps. Alligators are abundant in this section, but are seldom seen by noisy canoeists. During the summer, Ebenezer Creek is at its luxuriant best and is suggestive of a tropical rain forest. Insects abound, and birds, snakes, and turtles are common. The channel is more clearly defined at summer water levels and the fluted and swollen bases of bald cypresses and tupelos, as well as numerous bald cypress knees, are most obvious. In the fall the most striking change is in the color of the bald cypress needles.

Bald cypress is one of only a few deciduous conifers. The needles turn burnished copper and provide a beautiful color complement to the blue skies, white clouds, black water, and green of the other trees.

Mosquito fern forms huge floating mats on lower Ebenezer Creek, and during the short days of fall, winter, and early spring, the tiny leaves turn bright red.

There are three main put-in points for trips of about 5 miles each. Each segment provides a leisurely day of paddling with a stop for lunch and promises to captivate the casual visitor as well as the naturalist. The first section is from Georgia Highway 119 bridge to "Logs Landing" just off Georgia Highway 21, but this trip should not be attempted during low water. Ignore the unsightly midpoint bridge and enjoy a picnic at the 40-foot bluff on the right about half a mile beyond. The take-out is at Logs Landing just a half mile off Georgia Highway 21 on a dirt road at the Georgia historical marker for Old Ebenezer Town. The second section of about 4 miles begins at Logs Landing and ends at Long Bridge on Georgia Highway 953, 1.2 miles northwest of Georgia Highway 275. This section is also narrow and often blocked at low water, but is canoeable at moderate levels. The first half consists of a well-defined channel between low banks. A railroad bridge two-thirds of the way marks the start of a beautiful bald cypress swamp that contains areas of virgin timber. A good take-out occurs upstream of Long Bridge, but the landing is small, and one should park out of the way. The third and last section is the one usually chosen for summertime paddling. It is 5.5 miles long and ends at Ebenezer Landing on the Savannah River. The outstanding bald cypress swamp on the second section can be viewed by first paddling upstream about half a mile before starting downstream. Don't be fooled by the short mileage. It takes most people a day to enjoy this section to the fullest. This section contains one of the best developed tupelo swamps in the state. Paddling among the greatly swollen bases of 100 foot tall tupelos is an experience that is not soon forgotten. Below this point, the current is soon lost in the broad river swamp of the Savannah River. The take-out is on the right bank of the Savannah River at the site of New Ebenezer.

Suggested day trips:
- 5 miles - GA Hwy. 119 to Logs Landing (off GA Hwy. 21)
- 4 miles - Logs Landing to Long Bridge (GA Hwy. 953 off GA Hwy. 275)
- 5.5 miles - Long Bridge to Ebenezer Landing (Savannah River)

OGEECHEE RIVER

The Ogeechee River is born in Greene County where it begins as a tiny spring-fed trickle, but soon becomes a full grown river.

It flows for 245 miles before it empties into the Atlantic Ocean and is the state's longest river. The only dam is near Mayfield, and it powers a grist mill that is still in operation. In its upper reaches, the Ogeechee tumbles over shoals that offer challenge to white-water canoeists and provide suitable habitat for fish. Further south, the river breaks up into a series of bald cypress and tupelo swamps where wildlife abounds. Boaters unfamiliar with the area may find themselves lost in the swamps if they are not careful, for there are many blind-alley channels and little flow.

Downstream the river becomes serpentine and rushes around corners, through narrows, past high sand bluffs, then swings lazily around white sandbars that offer camping and picnic spots. Now and again the river widens into a "lake" and fishermen are almost always seen seeking the Ogeechee's fine fish.

Eventually the river becomes tidal below Safari Campground. Due to its great length the Ogeechee is like several separate rivers, each section having its own characteristics and sanctuaries for plants and animals.

A quiet canoeist may observe deer, otters, mink, beavers, several species of turtles and snakes, and a variety of frogs and salamanders. There are osprey nesting in view of the river; and a variety of songbirds, woodpeckers, ducks and wading birds make their home in the swamps and sloughs. The Ogeechee hosts a large variety of insect species including species of stone flies that probably have never been named. In addition, there are several endangered or protected plant species and some which are rare. Among these are pitcher plants, witch-alder, spider lily, and needle palm. The Ogeechee even boasts its own namesake tree – "Ogeechee lime." Its bright red fruits may be seen floating in quiet eddies in the fall. In the spring the canoeist may be treated to an array of fragrant wild azaleas. The Ogeechee is easily canoeable most of the year from Midville to the Safari Campground on Georgia Highway 204. Below this point the paddler must contend with tidal flow, and incorrect reckoning may result in bucking the incoming tide.

In late summer and fall when water is low, fallen logs and sandbars may require short easy portages, but during spring flood the Ogeechee becomes a high volume, fast flowing torrent best left to ducks and fish.

For hundreds of years Indians living in this area used the spot now known as Ogeechee Canal at the entrance to Safari Campground to ford the river. The river is broad and shallow even at high tide, and there is little current. The high banks offer dry ground on either side of the river.

When Oglethorpe came from England to establish Georgia as a colony, his first action was to protect access points into the colony. The old Indian trail that crossed the Ogeechee River became a major road from the south into Savannah. On the banks of the Ogeechee, Oglethorpe established Fort Argyle to protect the fledgling colony from Indians and the Spanish who controlled Florida. Later, Fort Argyle became a brick factory. Today it lies within the boundaries of Fort Stewart.

As the river meanders, straight canals run perpendicular to the river. These are evidence of the rice and indigo industry that prevailed during the early plantation period. The canals are now popular fishing haunts.

Favorite canoe trips of local paddlers are from Steel Bridge (Georgia Highway 119) to Dashers (U.S. Highway 80), from Dashers to Morgan's Bridge (Georgia Highway 204), or from Morgan's Bridge to Bellaire Woods Campground. The campground is reached by making a left turn into an old branch of the river 9.8 miles downstream. The turn is usually marked by a sign indicating the route into the fish camp located at the campground.

Suggested trips:

- 9.1 miles - GA Hwy. 56 (Midville) to County road 191 (Herndon)
- 15.7 miles - County road 191 to U.S. Hwy. 25 (Millen)
- 11 miles - U.S. Hwy. 25 to County road 190 (off GA Hwy. 17 at Scarboro)
- 6.5 miles - County road 190 to County road 57A (Rocky Ford)
- 7 miles - County road 57A to County road 581 (Ogeechee)
- 6.2 miles - County road 581 to U.S. Hwy. 301 (Dover)
- 15.2 miles - U.S. Hwy. 301 to GA Hwy. 24 (Oliver)
- 23.2 miles - GA Hwy. 24 to GA Hwy. 119 (Guyton)

- 12 miles - GA Hwy. 119 to U.S. Hwy. 80 (Dashers) at Blitchton
- 11.8 miles - U.S. Hwy. 80 to GA 204 (Morgan's Bridge)
- 9.8 miles - GA Hwy. 204 to Bellaire Woods Campground (off 204)
- 5.4 miles - Bellaire Woods Campground to U.S. Hwy. 17 (Kings Ferry)
- 7 miles - U.S. Hwy. 17 to GA Hwy. 144 (Rabbit Hill)
- 11.8 miles - GA Hwy. 144 to Spur 144 (Ft. McAllister)

ST. MARYS RIVER

The St. Marys River is a stream of quiet beauty. While canoeing its winding course, the paddler gets a true sense of being in a wilderness sanctuary. A feeling of peacefulness and serenity prevails here.

The St. Marys is 125 miles long and originates in the Okefenokee Swamp. The North Prong of the St. Marys flows south along the edge of Trail Ridge, which is the ancient dune line that forms the eastern border of the Okefenokee Swamp. There are several minor tributaries that feed the St. Marys. The first, and probably the most important, is the Middle Prong which rises in the Pinhook Swamp in northern Baker County, Florida. The Middle Prong flows east to join the St. Marys about two miles below the Florida Highway 120 bridge.

At this point the river widens and becomes a series of curves and sandbars as it flows to the sea. At the southern tip of Trail

Ridge the South Prong joins the river across from Charlton County, Georgia. Other minor tributaries, such as Cedar Creek, Spanish Creek, Little St. Marys River, and North River, contribute to the river's volume. With the exception of a few houses at the confluence of South Prong, there are virtually no buildings or structures. Between Georgia Highway 301 and the mouth of the St. Marys, motorboats are prevalent and intrude upon the quiet wilderness.

From its origin, the St. Marys is lined with stately, moss-draped bald cypress trees and sculptured trunks of tupelos and Ogeechee lime trees. As the river flows east from the Highway 301 bridge, the tidal influence becomes evident. On one side of the river the bald cypress and tupelo remain, while on the other side marsh appears. Further downriver, marsh prevails on both sides and, depending on the stage of the tide, the current can be swift or nonexistent.

An abundance of wildlife can be seen by those who are quiet and observant. In the spring, swallow-tailed and Mississippi kites might be spotted. Red-shouldered and red-tailed hawks, as well as osprey and night herons, can be seen most times of the year. During the spring migration, small songbirds flit back and forth across the river. Wading birds of various kinds can be seen near the mouth of the river. For the very lucky, a white-tailed deer, raccoon, opossum, armadillo, or alligator might appear.

In the past, the St. Marys was of particular importance to ocean-going mariners. The burgundy red water of this river is clearer than most river water, probably because its primary source is the Okefenokee Swamp. The tannic acid from decaying vegetation in the swamp and river is responsible for the dark tea color. The acid acts as a preservative as well, and for this reason ocean sailing ships went out of their way to obtain water from the St. Marys.

There are many good access points to the St. Marys, and it is a river easily canoed by the novice. The numerous sandbars provide good campsites at most water levels. Several day trips or longer overnight camping trips are possible.

Suggested trips:
- 5.14 miles - GA Hwy. 94 (Moniac) to FL Hwy. 120
- 12.4 miles - FL Hwy. 120 to GA Hwy. 23
- 9.6 miles - GA Hwy. 23 to Stokes Bridge
- 13.7 miles - Stokes Bridge to GA Hwy. 94 (St. George)
- 27.5 miles - GA Hwy. 94 (St. George) to Traders Hill Landing
- 7.7 miles - Traders Hill to White Springs Landing (Camp Pickney Park)
- 26.3 miles - White Springs to U.S. Hwy. 17

Canoe Outposts in Hilliard, FL provides shuttles and rents canoes and gear (904/536-7928).

SATILLA RIVER

The Satilla River is another delightful blackwater stream that arises on the coastal plain. Its waters are clear and dark, and much of the riverbed is clean white sand. The Satilla River originates in Ben Hill and Coffee counties at an elevation of only 350 feet, and it flows gently east for about 260 miles before emptying into St. Andrews Sound. The Satilla has several major tributaries that offer additional canoeing possibilities in the spring: Big and Little Satilla Creeks join to form the Little Satilla River, and Big and Little Hurricane Creeks join to form the Alapaha River. The 149 mile stretch from Waycross (U.S. Hwy. 82) to the ocean offers the most reliable canoeing, but the sections between put-in and take-out points are lengthy. Most paddlers would probably prefer overnight trips on all sections except U.S. Hwy. 82/GA Hwy. 15.

The Satilla is one of the few remaining wilderness rivers in the state, although second home development along the lower stretches is becoming obvious. Early trappers used to bring bales of fur out of the Satilla country, and it is still renowned for its wildlife. Animals frequently seen include squirrel, raccoon, deer, alligator, duck, and an occasional wild turkey. The river is renowned for largemouth bass, crappie, red-breast and bream. The upper portions of the river and its tributaries are bounded by a typical bottomland swamp of bald cypress, tupelo, and sweetbay magnolia. Higher hills or ridges support various oaks and pines. Between Waycross and the sea, the water shed is comprised mostly of managed timberlands. The high sandy flats are covered with pines, and the lower areas are covered by bald cypress, tupelos, and hardwoods. The banks are sandy and well defined often reaching 8 feet or more in height. Large white sandbars are particularly common along this river and make ideal campsites during most seasons. At high water there are plenty of high sandy bluffs for camping. History buffs may want to walk to the site of Burnt Fort (just above the GA Hwy. 252 bridge), a pre-Revolutionary era fort.

Suggested trips:
- 15.7 miles - U.S. Hwy. 82 to GA Hwys. 15 and 121
- 26.8 miles - GA Hwys. 15 and 121 to U.S. Hwy. 301
- 20.2 miles - U.S. Hwy. 301 to U.S. Hwy. 84
- 35.3 miles - U.S. Hwy. 84 to GA Hwy. 252 (Burnt Fort)
- 24.5 miles - GA Hwy. 252 to U.S. Hwy. 17

SAVANNAH RIVER

The Savannah River, starting at the confluence of the Tugaloo and Seneca Rivers in Hart County, forms the boundary between Georgia and South Carolina. It was once a majestic, free-flowing river, but is now dammed in many places for hydro-electric generation. Although dams have obstructed, altered, and tamed much of the river, there remain long stretches below Augusta that seem relatively wild. Along its banks and on its islands there still stand magnificent trees. Towering bald cypress trees are most easily recognized from the passing canoe, but there also are oaks, maples, hickories, and tupelos. The first major tributary below U.S. Hwy. 301 is Brier Creek, a river that deserves exploration in its own right. Given the time, skill, and strength to paddle upstream on Brier Creek a half-mile or so, the canoeist will find the banks crowded with the blue-fruited dogwood and may catch a glimpse of the beautiful wood duck.

On the Georgia side are high banks and sometimes imposing bluffs on which can be found the beautiful flame azalea as well as a variety of other plants belonging to the more northerly piedmont flora. A good example is the native mountain laurel that survives near Sister's Ferry, a river crossing near the early settlement of Purysburg, South Carolina. Below Sister's Ferry, the canoeist will pass the mouth of Ebenezer Creek, and may wish to paddle a short distance up this historic creek. The ruins of bridge pilings from an ancient bridge may still be visible. Here travelers such as John and William Bartram crossed on their journeys, and here, too, passed the British in the American Revolution and Sherman's men in the Civil War. Along the creek banks are tupelo trees standing tall with an obvious twist in their bark that offers an ecological puzzle. Near the mouth of the creek one might see an interesting vine, American buckwheat vine, and along the walk from the landing up to the historic church of the Salzburgers may be found red buckeye. The church and the museum at New Ebenezer are well worth the time spent ashore.

Soon the canoeist may come upon the white spider lily in the swampy margins of the river. The paddler with a taste for history may know that this area was once the site of old rice plantations. Among them is the old Nathanael Greene plantation,

Mulberry Grove, where Eli Whitney built his original cotton gin. At last, the river enters the industrial and shipping areas of Savannah, and the journey ends unless the canoeist elects to travel downstream past Tybee Island to the sea. If the river could tell its stories, they would be many and fascinating. One day in a canoe on the river, and the paddler will sense and feel its spell and be drawn back again and again.

The Savannah River is a large, powerful river in its lower reaches and should be approached with caution. The best season for canoeing is during the summer and fall when the water levels are at their lowest and the water is warm. Power boating is common, and occasionally commercial barges travel up the river to Augusta. Lifejackets are recommended at all times on this river. Local landings are fairly common, but usually one must ask local residents where these locations are, and a fee is charged at some of them. A full day's canoe trip is from Tuckassee King Landing about 3 miles above Clyo, to Ebenezer Landing at the north end of Georgia Highway 275. This trip is about 22 miles, but the current of the river helps considerably. A shorter trip of about 13 miles is from Ebenezer Landing to Purysburg Landing in South Carolina. From Purysburg Landing it is about 16.5 miles to the U.S. Highway 17 bridge and a public ramp. The canoeist should remember to allow for the tide in this section.

SUWANNEE RIVER

The most famous of all Southern rivers, the Suwannee, lives up to the images created by Stephen C. Foster in his song,

"Swanee River." Certainly, the Suwannee is a river of beauty, but the unique feature of the Suwannee is her source.

The headwaters of the Suwannee lie deep within the Okefenokee Swamp. Near Billy's Island two waterways join forces, and it is generally accepted that the Suwannee begins at this confluence. The river flows southwest from Billy's Island for 250 miles before spilling into the Gulf of Mexico. The Suwannee drains the Okefenokee to the west and is the major outlet for the swamp's voluminous water supply.

The best way to enjoy the magic of the Suwannee is to begin at the headwaters. Stephen C. Foster State Park is an easy access point and is open to all. By paddling out of the boat basin and into Billy's Lake, the second mile of the Suwannee River is reached. Paddling a few miles further southwest brings the canoeist to the River Narrows; the river does indeed narrow here. This is a fascinating three miles through fetter bush, tupelo trees, smilax vines, and bald cypress stumps. The area was heavily logged in the early 1900's. As the paddler winds through this channel, a large open area is reached with many lily pads where alligators often bask in the sun. After crossing this area, the channel becomes a narrow passageway that is lined totally with tupelo trees that have much parasitic American mistletoe in their high canopies. A bit further on the paddler's progress will be blocked by a long earthen sill or dike with spillways.

This sill was built in the 1950's after the last great fires in the Okefenokee to help maintain more constant water level throughout the year. On the other side of the sill the Suwannee continues. Paddlers must have a permit from the Okefenokee National Wildlife Refuge to cross the sill. The canoes must be portaged around the spillways.

Once the canoeist crosses the sill, the Suwannee becomes more like a river except during high spring water. In spring the Suwannee usually spills over its banks from an accumulation of rainwater, which raises the level of the swamp and ultimately the level of the river. When the river is high, the current is deceptively smooth but swift. During this flood stage the river's main course can be difficult to follow in places. For the most part, the canoeist is paddling through the trees. Watch the flow of the current and head in a southwesterly direction.

After crossing the sill it is about six miles to a takeout point at Griffis Fish Camp (Route 1, Box 139, Fargo, GA 31631; telephone 912/637-5395) (watch for a sign on the left). Permission must be obtained from the fish camp to take out here, and a fee may be charged. The fish camp may also run prearranged shuttles for a fee. Camping is also permitted by reservation. The land is owned by the Griffis family who has lived here since the 1850's, so one may want to take advantage of their wealth of knowledge of local natural and human history.

There are other takeout points before the Fargo Bridge, but they are on private property and permission must be obtained to use these access points. The Fargo Bridge at river mile 13.1 has a public boat ramp.

181

The next good takeout and camping spot is Touchton's Camp (C. W. Smith, Route 1, Fargo, GA 31631; telephone 912/637-5363). The camp must be contacted in advance for permission to put in, take out, or camp. The camp also charges a fee for these privileges.

From the sill to Touchton's the river has a magical quality that is enhanced by the majestic bald cypress trees with their fluted buttressed trunks. At times other than flood stage, enchanting gnome-like bald cypress knees line the banks, and they seem to sit in review as the canoeists form a flotilla parade. The tupelos also lend magic to the river with their oddly shaped trunks.

Below Touchton's Camp the next access point, Rolane's Landing, is across the Florida state line, and just six miles below that is the Florida Highway 6 bridge that is a good take-out spot. From Touchton's on down, limestone outcroppings and higher banks become noticeable.

For most of the year, except during spring flooding there are numerous sandbars on which to camp. During high water, however, saw palmettos and pine trees indicate high ground. The wildlife is abundant on the Suwannee, but one must be quiet and pay attention. Otters play along the river banks, and with some luck one might catch a glimpse of this delightful creature.

From the Florida Highway 6 bridge, the Suwannee courses its way over 200 miles southwestward through Florida to empty into the Gulf of Mexico near Cedar Key.

THE GEORGIA CONSERVANCY

Coastal Marine Habitat

The Georgia Conservancy is an independent, statewide, nonprofit organization which actively works on improving the quality of the environment. The organization was founded in 1967, a product of the combined efforts of Robert Hanie, a Georgia idealist desiring to conserve the natural beauty of his home state, and James Mackey, a U.S. Congressman interested in the hot political issue of the environment.

Citizens sharing the concern of these two men banded together under the name of The Georgia Conservancy and began to address environmental problems in the state of Georgia. The organization had its base in Atlanta. In 1972, under the stewardship of the Junior League of Savannah, a coastal office was established in Savannah under the leadership of Hans Neuhauser. The Georgia Conservancy began a true statewide campaign as a "watchdog" or "guardian angel" to protect and conserve natural resources in Georgia.

As its goals, The Georgia Conservancy seeks to protect and enhance the quality of Georgia's environment and to encourage wise use of the state's natural resources. To achieve this, professional staff and volunteers work toward finding a balance between the needs of the state's economy, the social and cultural needs of its people, and the needs of natural systems trying to maintain their vital functions.

Education and advocacy are the basic tools of The Georgia Conservancy. The group first educates itself through research into all sides of the issues. The board of trustees then seeks the most responsible and effective approach. Advocacy methods include direct contact with decision-makers, statements at public hearings, programs in the news media, educational publications, seminars, field trips, luncheon meetings, and *A Guide to the Georgia Coast*. Whenever possible, the Conservancy seeks to solve environmental problems by means of positive, cooperative programs rather than by adversarial confrontation. If necessary, the organization will litigate, but this step has seldom been required.

Through the coastal office of The Georgia Conservancy, staff and members have advocated protection for beaches and dunes, marshlands, endangered species, Okefenokee Swamp Wilderness, Cumberland Island National Seashore and Wilderness Area, Sapelo Island National Estuarine Research Reserve, the Ogeechee River, Blackbeard Island National Wildlife Refuge and Wilderness Area, Georgia Heritage Trust Program, Gray's Reef National Marine Sanctuary, and Harris Neck National Wildlife Refuge. The coastal office has influenced decisions on resources, selective industrial development for coastal Georgia, improved environmental protection for offshore oil development, living with barrier islands, oil spill cleanup, coastal management, National Park Service planning, and linking harbor maintenance with beach renourishment.

The Georgia Conservancy continues to reflect both the love of nature and a pragmatic approach in conserving natural resources. It is the function of this organization, working with many others in the public and private sector, to protect sensitive ecosystems and to reduce the long-range effects of man's intervention.

This Appendix gives charter services, boat ramps, fish camps, marinas, and canoe outfitters according to our geographical divisions of the sites. Information current as of 1984.

Northern Coast
Charter Services

Captain Boat Name	Address and Telephone	Offshore	Inshore	Bottom	Trolling	Diving	Gulf Stream	Fee
Captain Judy Helmey "Miss Judy Too!" Captain Bill Marsh "Miss Judy" Captain Sherman Helmey "Miss Jerry"	1009 Tara Ave. (mailing) 124 Palmetto Ave. (Boats) Savannah, GA 31410 (912) 897-4921	•	•	•	•	•	•	$200-$700
Captain Chris Morse "Reel Love"	1147 Shawnee St. Savannah, GA 31406 (912) 925-9030 or 925-5637	•		•	•	•	•	$250-$700
Neva-Miss Charter Boats Gloria Shearin 7 boats	2 Cedar Point Savannah, GA 31410 (912) 897-2706	•	•	•	•	•	•	$194-$375
Coffee Bluff Fish Camp	14915 White Bluff Rd. Savannah, GA 31419 (912) 925-9030	•	•	•	•	•	•	$150-$600
Captain Jim Newman "Adventurer III"	Offshore Adventure Co. 409 Montgomery Crossroads Savannah, GA 31406 927-4516 or 354-0162	•	•	•	•		•	$200-$600
Captain Mark Covington "Adventurer"	Offshore Adventure Co. Wormsloe-Isle of Hope Savannah, GA 31406 354-9651	•	•	•	•			$200-$400
Captain Emmet Bridges	114-A Palmetto Dr. Savannah, GA 31410 (912) 897-2694	•	•	•	•	•	•	$275-$700
Captain David Avant "Un-Reel"	P.O. Box 189 Richmond Hill, GA 31324 (912) 727-2470	•	•	•	•			$125-$250

Public Boat Ramps
Chatham County
- Bells Landing – Apache Street, off Abercorn St., on Hoover Creek
- Island Expressway – East of bridge on Wilmington River
- King's Ferry Park – U.S. Hwy. 17 South. Ogeechee River

- Lake Mayer – Off Montgomery Crossroads, before Skidaway Road
- Lazaretto Creek – U.S. Hwy. 80 to Tybee Island at Lazaretto Creek
- Montgomery – One-half mile from the end of Whitfield Ave. South Vernon River
- Port Wentworth – U.S. Hwy. 17 North (old bridge) on Front River
- Savannah National Wildlife Refuge – Off U.S. Hwy. 17 north on Back River
- Silk Hope – Old U.S. Hwy. 17 South at Salt Creek
- Skidaway Narrows – Diamond Causeway at the Narrows on Skidaway River
- Thunderbolt – U.S. Hwy. 80 on Armstrong Island (Savannah Marina) on Wilmington River
- Tybee – On Tybee Island, 16th Street. Back River

Bryan County

- Canoochee Park – On GA Hwy. 30 at Canoochee River at Evans/Bryan County line
- Demeries Creek – Southeast of Hwy. 17 on GA 144 at DNR Game and Fish Regional office on Demeries Creek
- Morgan Bridge – On GA Hwy. 204 at Ogeechee River on Chatham/Bryan County line
- Richmond Hill State Park – Southeast of Hwy. 17 on GA 144 Spur. At fork, go left to end of spur. One is on Ogeechee River; another is on Red Bird Creek.

Fish Camps and Marinas

Chatham County

- Bandy's Bait and Tackle – 355-5451. 7012 LaRoche Ave. on Herb River (Bait, food and ice)
- Bellaire Woods Campgrounds – 748-7634. Northwest off GA 204, just past Savannah and Ogeechee Canal on left. Ogeechee River. (Bait, camping, charter service, food and ice, fuel, boat ramp)

- Bona Bella Marina – 355-9601. Livingston Avenue at Williamson Creek
- Chimney Creek Fishing Camp – 786-9857. Tybee Island, south of U.S. Hwy. 80 on Chimney Creek. (Hoist, bait, camping, charter service, food and ice, and fuel)
- Coffee Bluff Fish Camp – 925-9962. Coffee Bluff Road at Forest River. (Hoist, charter service, food and ice, and fuel)
- Fountain Marina – 354-2283. 2812 River Drive, Thunderbolt. (Hoist, bait, camping, food and ice, and fuel)
- Harrison's Fishing Camp – 355-0232. Off Shipyard Road on Shipyard Creek. Boat rental only.
- Isle of Hope Marina – 355-2310. Off Skidaway Road at Isle of Hope on Skidaway River. (Hoist, fuel)
- Lazaretto Boat Club – 897-9974. Off Wilmington Island Road on Wilmington River. For boat club members only.
- Love's Fishing Camp – 925-2232. On U.S. Hwy. 17 South at Ogeechee River
- Sail Harbor – 897-2896. Wilmington Island on Turners Creek (Hoist, charter service, food and ice)
- Tidewater Boat Works, Inc. – 352-1335. North of U.S. Hwy. 80 in Thunderbolt. Wilmington River. (Hoist, charter service, food and ice, and fuel)
- Turner's Creek Marina – 897-5495. Off GA 367 at Turner Creek. (Hoist, bait, charter service, food and ice, fuel)
- Tuten's Fishing Camp – 355-9182. Off LaRoche Avenue at Herb River. (Hoist, bait, food and ice, fuel)
- Tybee Island Marina – 786-4996. Southwest side of Tybee Island on Tybee Creek. (Hoist, bait, food and ice, fuel)
- Young's Marina – 897-2608. 218 Wilmington Road. (Hoist, bait, food and ice)

Bryan County

- Dashers Fishing Lodge – No phone. On U.S. Hwy. 80 on Ogeechee River at Bryan/Effingham County line.
- Kilkenny Fish Camp – 727-2215. Take GA 144 southeast from

U.S. Hwy. 17, turn left on Kilkenny Road. Go to dead end. Kilkenny Creek. (Hoist, bait, camping, charter service, food and ice, fuel)
- Ogeechee Marine Center – 756-2426. On U.S. Hwy. 17 on Ogeechee River at Bryan/Chatham County line.

Central Coast Charter Services

Captain Boat Name	Address and Telephone	Offshore	Inshore	Bottom	Trolling	Diving	Gulf Stream	Fee
Kip's Fish Camp	Townsend, GA 31331 (912) 832-5162	•	•	•	•			Negotiable
Fisherman's Lodge	Townsend, GA 31331 (912) 832-4671	•	•	•	•			$360-$600
Captain Kent Hutchison "Fishing Fever" Captain Tim Tarver "Sapelo Jack" Captain Fred Daniels "Sea Venture"								

Public Boat Ramps
McIntosh County
- Champney Island – Turn west off U.S. Hwy. 17 on south side of Champney River Bridge.
- Darien – On U.S. Hwy. 17, north of first traffic light in Darien. Turn left, ramp is one-half block down, on left, on Altamaha River.
- Harper Lake – At Harper Lake on Altamaha River off GA 251 past Cox.
- Old Fort Barrington – At Old Fort Barrington on Altamaha River off GA 251 past Cox.
- Ridgeville (public docks) – Off GA 99 at Ridgeville on North River.

- White Chimney – On Shellman Bluff Road at second White Chimney River Bridge.

Liberty County
- Sunbury – East on Interstate 95, off GA 38 on Drum Point Landing turn off. Newport River is before the landing.

Fish Camps and Marinas
McIntosh County
- Belle Bluff Island Marina – 832-5323. East of U.S. Hwy. 17 between Pine Harbor and Shellman Bluff on White River. (Hoist, bait, camping, charter service, food and ice, fuel)
- Blackbeard Cove Marina – 437-4878. Off GA 99 at Ridgeville on North River. (Hoist, bait, charter service, food and ice, fuel)
- Fisherman's Lodge – 832-4671. East of Hwy. 17 at Shellman Bluff on Broad River.
- Harris Neck Fish Camp – 832-4603. East of Hwy. 17 on Harris Neck Road past end of GA 131 on dirt road at Swain River. (Hoist, bait, charter service, food and ice, fuel)
- Kip's Fishing Camp – 832-5162. East of U.S. Hwy. 17 at Shellman Bluff on Broad River. (Hoist, bait, camping, charter service, food and ice, fuel)
- McIntosh County Rod and Gun Club – 437-4677. Off GA 99 at Ridgeville on North River. (Hoist, food and ice, fuel)
- Pine Harbor Marina – 832-5886. East of Hwy. 17 at Pine Harbor on Belleville River. (Hoist, bait, food and ice, fuel)

Liberty County
- Half Moon Marina – 884-5819. East of Interstate 95, off GA 38 on Drum Point Landing turn off. Newport River before the landing. (Hoist, bait, camping, food and ice, fuel)
- Lake George – No phone. Between U.S. 17 and Interstate 95 on Gress River approximately 1 mile from Liberty/Bryan County line.
- Yellow Bluff Fishing Camp – 884-5448. East of Interstate 95 on GA 38 at dead end. (Hoist, bait, food and ice, fuel)

Southern Coast Charter Services

Captain Boat Name	Address and Telephone	Offshore	Inshore	Bottom	Trolling	Diving	Gulf Stream	Fee
Seecruise "Island Queen"	911 Bay Street Brunswick, GA 31520 (912) 265-1471	•	•				•	$900-$1200
Inland Charter Boat Service	N. 1st Street Sea Island, GA 31561 (912) 638-3611, ext. 202			•	•			$60-$147.50
Captain Frank Mead	(912) 638-4261							
Captain Tracy Youmans	638-2308							
Captain Jim Geeslin	638-2900							
Captain David Blackshear	638-2512 or 638-8132							
Captain Sam Drury	638-7857							
Captain Charlie Grittis	638-3611							
Captain Jay Childers	638-2483							
Cap Fendig Charter Boats	P.O. Box 1715 St. Simons Island, GA 31522 (912) 638-7717	•		•	•	•	•	$235-$450
Captain Cap Fendig "Gone Fishing" Captain Bob Watts "Sparrow" Captain Jack Hicks "Cracker Jack"	Inshore fishing between 9AM and 3PM $25 per hr. Boat rentals 2-hour minimum. Party boat fishing from May 1st until Labor Day. Also sailboat rentals.							
Two Way Fish Camp	Route 2, Box 84 Darien Highway Brunswick, GA 31520 (912) 264-9723	•	•	•	•	•		$110-$450
Tradewinds Fleet (party fishing boat, call for weekly schedule) also: 1 six-man boat 1 four-man boat 1 boat for inshore fishing	Jekyll Island Marina 1 Pier Road Jekyll Island, GA 31520 (912) 635-2891	•	•	•	•		•	12 hr. $38.00. Sr. citizen, military & under 12 - $3.00 discount. Prices vary
Captain Ray Potter "Dolphin"	Route 6, Box 330 Brunswick, GA 31520 (912) 267-7494, 265-1996	•	•	•	•	•	•	$300-$600
Captain Danny Drummond	706 Oak Lane Brunswick, GA 31520 (912) 264-1733		•	•				Negotiable
Captain James McVeigh	(912) 264-9723		•	•				Negotiable
Captain Mike Evans "Wild Turkey"	48A Patton Drive Brunswick, GA 31520 (912) 264-9723	•	•	•	•	•	•	$100-$300
Captain Chip Bright "Wild Turkey" "Jet Lag"	(912) 264-9723 (912) 264-6834	•		•	•	•	•	

Captain Boat Name	Address and Telephone	Offshore	Inshore	Bottom	Trolling	Diving	Gulf Stream	Fee
Captain Chuck Hall "Magic II"	3110 Altama Avenue Brunswick, GA 31520 (912) 264-5461	•	•	•	•			Negotiable
Captain E. Maxwell Smith	130 Deerfield Drive Brunswick, GA 31520 (912) 265-8302	•	•	•	•	•	•	$100-$450
Captain Walter Hewitt	P.O. Box 593 Kingsland, GA 31548 (912) 729-5834	•	•	•	•			Negotiable
Kingfish Charters Captain C. C. Higginbotham	P.O. Box 444 Woodbine, GA 31569 (912) 576-5724	•	•	•	•			$150

Public Boat Ramps

Glynn County

- Altamaha Fish Camp – Northeast of U.S. Hwy. 341 at Everett on paved road. Approximately 1¼ miles to Altamaha River.
- Blythe Island – Turn right off GA 303 on Blythe Island Drive. Go past Interstate 95. Turn right on second road on right. Two ramps at end of the road on Turtle River.
- Harrington – On St. Simons Island, turn right off Frederica Road at the Red Barn, then go to dead end at Village Creek.
- MacKay River – On Torras Causeway at MacKay River.
- South Brunswick River – GA 303 at South Brunswick River.
- Turtle River – On GA 303 at Turtle River.

Camden County

- Burnt Fork (Charlton County) – On GA 252 at Camden/ Charlton County line. Satilla River.
- Crooked River State Park – East of Interstate 95, turn north on GA 40 Spur off GA 40. At dead end on Crooked River.
- Harriett's Bluff – East on Interstate 95 off Harriett's Bluff Road on Crooked River.
- Kingsland – On U.S. Hwy. 17 at St. Marys River, Georgia/ Florida line.
- Little Satilla River – On U.S. Hwy. 17 at the Little Satilla River Bridge.
- St. Marys – Take GA 40 to dead end in St. Marys. Turn right, ramp on left at St. Marys River.
- Satilla River – Off U.S. Hwy. 17 in Woodbine on Satilla River.
- White Oak – On U.S. Hwy. 17 at White Oak Creek.

Fish Camps and Marinas

Glynn County

- Brunswick Marina – (912) 265-2290. U.S. Hwy. 17 just south of Torras Causeway at Clubbs Creek and Terry Creek Basin. (Hoist, bait, food and ice, fuel)
- Golden Isles Marina – (912) 638-8633. On Torras Causeway at Frederica River. (Hoist, charter service, food and ice, and fuel)
- Jekyll Marina – (912) 635-2891. No. 1 Pier Road. (Hoist, bait, charter service, food and ice, and fuel)
- Harry Jones – (912) 265-1757. On GA 303 just north of Turtle River. (Hoist, bait)
- St. Simons Boating and Fishing Club – (912) 638-9146. On Gascoigne Bluff. Frederica River. (Hoist, food and ice, fuel)
- Speedy's Marina – (912) 265-7611. East of U.S. Hwy. 17 on Colonels Island at Jointer Creek. (Hoist, bait, food and ice)
- Taylor's Fish Camp – (912) 638-8201. On Lawrence Road. On St. Simons Island north on Frederica Road North. North of

German Village on Hampton River. (Hoist, bait, charter service)

- Troupe Creek Marina – (912) 264-3862. North on U.S. Hwy. 17 past Glynco traffic light. Turn right at marina sign. (Hoist, bait, charter service, food and ice, fuel)
- Two Way Fish Camp – (912) 264-9723. On U.S. 17 North at Altamaha River. (Hoist, bait, camping, charter service, food and ice, fuel)

Camden County
- Hickory Bluff Fish Camp – (912) 264-3458. East of Interstate 95 off Dover Bluff Road at Hickory Bluff on Little Satilla River. (Hoist, bait, charter service, food and ice, fuel)
- Hubert Barber – (912) 729-5051. East of Interstate 95 off Harriett's Bluff Road. (Bait, food and ice, fuel, and boat rentals)

- Jack's Marina – (912) 882-3227. East of Interstate 95, turn north on GA 40 Spur off GA 40. Go to dead end. Crooked River. (Bait, charter service, food and ice, and boat ramp)
- Lang – No phone. End of GA 40 in St. Marys, St. Marys River. Wet storage only.
- Ocean Breeze Campground – (912) 729-9945. East of Interstate 95 off Dover Bluff Road on Little Satilla River. (Hoist, bait, camping, charter service, food and ice, fuel)
- 3 R Fishing Camp – No phone. At the Camden/Charlton County line. Satilla River.
- Ray Pounds – (912) 729-5747. East of Interstate 95 off Harriett's Bluff Road. Crooked River. (Hoist, bait)

**Reprinted by permission from the Department of Natural Resources from *Coastlines Georgia,* Richard Daigle, Editor.

APPENDIX B

SELECTED READING

Balantine, Todd. Tideland Treasure. Deerfield Publishing, Inc. (1983).

Cheney, Brainard. River Rogue. Washington: Burr Oak Publishers. (1982).

Dean, L., Editor. The Value and Vulnerability of Coastal Resources. Georgia Department of Natural Resources. (1975).

Earl, John. John Muir's Longest Walk. New York: Doubleday & Co. (1975).

Hanie, Robert. Guale, The Golden Coast of Georgia. Seabury Press. (1974).

Harper, Francis and Delma E. Presley. Okefinoke Album. Athens: University of Georgia Press. (1981).

Harper, Francis. The Travels of William Bartram, Naturalists's Edition. Yale University Press. (1958).

Heyward, D.C. Seed from Madagascar. University of North Carolina Press. (1937).

Johnson, A.S., H.O. Hillestad, S.F. Shanholtzer and G.F. Shanholtzer. An Ecological Survey of the Coastal Region of Georgia. National Park Service Scientific Monograph Series No. 3. (1974).

Kemble, Fanny A. Journal of a Residence on a Georgian Plantation in 1838-1839. Athens: University of Georgia Press. (1984).

Kinsey, B. (1982) A Sapelo Island Handbook, University of Georgia Marine Institute, Sapelo Is.

Lewis, Bessie. They Called Their Town Darien. The Darien (Ga.) News. (1975).

Lovell, C. C. Golden Isles of Georgia. Little Co. (1932).

McKenzie, N. C., and L. A. Barclay. Ecological Characterization of the Sea Island Coastal Region of South Carolina and Georgia. U.S. Fish & Wildlife Service, Office of Biological Services. (1980).

Muir, John. A Thousand-Mile Walk to the Gulf. New York: Houghton Mifflin Co. (1916).

Myers, R.M., Editor. The Children of Pride. Yale University Press. (1972).

Price, Eugenia. St. Simons Triology: The Beloved Intruder (1965), New Moon Rising (1969) and Lighthouse (1971). Lippincott.

Russel, Francis. The Okefenokee Swamp. The American Wilderness/Time-Life Books. (1973).

Schoettle, H. E. Taylor. A Field Guide to Jekyll Island. Marine Extension Service, University of Georgia. (1983).

Scruggs, C. P. Georgia Historical Markers. Bay Tree Grove Publishers. (1973).

Sehlinger, Bob, and Don Otey. Southern Georgia Canoeing. Thomas Press. (1980).

Teal, J., and M. Teal. Life and Death of the Salt Marsh. Ballentine. (1969).

Teal, J., and M. Teal. Portrait of an Island. Athens: University of Georgia Press. (1981).

Van Doren, Mark, Editor. Travels of William Bartram. Dover Publications, Inc. (1928).

Vanstory, Burnette. Georgia's Land of the Golden Isles. University of Georgia Press. (1981).

Wharton, Charles H. The Natural Environments of Georgia. Georgia Department of Natural Resources. (1978).

INDEX

You Are Invited To Become A Member

Promote environmental quality in Georgia. As a member, you will help to:

- Develop and influence growth management strategies for our rapidly developing state

- Strengthen regulations which guard Georgia's air and water

- Complete the popular Chattahoochee River National Recreation Area

- Ensure efficient and safe energy sources for Georgia's future

- Protect Georgia's forests and natural areas from unwise development, improper harvesting methods, or misuse of chemicals

- Work for protection of river corridors and barrier islands in Georgia

- Increase awareness for Georgia's new nongame species programs

Yes, count me in as a partner in The Georgia Conservancy:

Name _____

Address _____

City _____ County _____

State _____ Zip _____

Phone: (H) _____ (W) _____

Occupation_____
(Students: Please give school name and class)

Business/Organization _____

Spouse Name_____

Spouse Occupation _____

Spouse Bus./Org. _____

Spouse Work Phone _____

☐ Please contact me about volunteer opportunities.

Please make check payable to The Georgia Conservancy and return to:

The Georgia Conservancy 8615 Barnwell Rd., Alpharetta, GA 30201

☐ Gold Cambium†	$1,000 or more
☐ Silver Cambium†	$500 or more
☐ Bronze Cambium†	$250 or more
☐ Donor	$100 or more
☐ Sustaining	$70
☐ Nonprofit Organization	$40
☐ Family	$40
☐ Individual*	$25
☐ Retired	$15
☐ Student*	$15

† *Qualifies for special events.*

*Per Person. All other categories cover individuals and/or families.